The Mastaba of Ptahhetep and Akhethetep at Saqqareh, Volume 8

Francis Llewellyn Griffith, Norman Garis De Davies

PTAH-HETEP

(from the east wall of his chapel)

ARCHAEOLOGICAL SURVEY OF EGYPT

EDITED BY F. LL. GRIFFITH.

EIGHTH MEMOIR

THE MASTABA OF
PTAHHETEP AND AKHETHETEP

AT SAQQAREH

PART I.

THE CHAPEL OF PTAHHETEP AND THE HIEROGLYPHS

BY

N. DE G. DAVIES, M.A., B.D.

WITH CHAPTERS BY THE EDITOR

THIRTY-ONE PLATES, THREE COLOURED

SPECIAL PUBLICATION OF THE EGYPT EXPLORATION FUND

LONDON
SOLD AT
THE OFFICES OF THE EGYPT EXPLORATION FUND, 37, GREAT RUSSELL STREET, W.C
AND AT 59, TEMPLE STREET, BOSTON, MASS., U.S.A.
AND BY KEGAN PAUL, TRENCH, TRÜBNER & CO., PATERNOSTER HOUSE, CHARING CROSS ROAD, W.C.
B. QUARITCH, 15, PICCADILLY, W.; ASHER & CO., 13, BEDFORD STREET, COVENT GARDEN, W.C.

1900

LONDON :
PRINTED BY GILBERT AND RIVINGTON, LIMITED,
ST. JOHN'S HOUSE, CLERKENWELL.

EGYPT EXPLORATION FUND.

President.

SIR JOHN EVANS, K.C.B., D.C.L., LL.D., F.R.S.

Vice=Presidents.

SIR E. MAUNDE-THOMPSON, K.C.B., D.C.L., LL.D.

LT.-GENERAL SIR FRANCIS GRENFELL, G.C.M.G., G.C.B.

THE REV. PROF. A. H. SAYCE, M.A., LL.D.

CHARLES DUDLEY WARNER, Esq., L.H.D., LL.D. (U.S.A.).

THE REV. W. C. WINSLOW, D.D., D.C.L. (U.S.A.).

THE HON. CHAS. L. HUTCHINSON (U.S.A.).

PROF. G. MASPERO, D.C.L. (France).

PROF. AD. ERMAN, Ph.D. (Germany).

JOSIAH MULLENS, Esq. (Australia).

M. CHARLES HENTSCH (Switzerland).

Hon. Treasurers.

H. A. GRUEBER, Esq., F.S.A.   F. C. FOSTER, Esq. (Boston, U.S.A.).

Hon. Secretaries.

J. S. COTTON, Esq., M.A.   THE REV. W. C. WINSLOW, D.D., D.C.L. (Boston, U.S.A.)

Members of Committee.

T. H. BAYLIS, Esq., M.A., Q.C., V.D.

MISS M. BRODRICK, Ph.D. (for Boston).

SOMERS CLARKE, Esq., F.S.A.

W. E. CRUM, Esq., M.A.

ARTHUR JOHN EVANS, Esq., M.A., F.S.A.

F. LL. GRIFFITH, Esq., M.A., F.S.A.

MRS. F. LL. GRIFFITH.

T. FARMER HALL, Esq.

JOHN HORNIMAN, Esq., M.P.

F. G. KENYON, Esq., M.A., LITT.D.

MRS. MCCLURE.

THE REV. W. MACGREGOR, M.A.

A. S. MURRAY, Esq., LL.D., F.S.A.

THE MARQUIS OF NORTHAMPTON.

FRANCIS WM. PERCIVAL, Esq., M.A., F.S.A.

PROF. W. M. FLINDERS PETRIE, D.C.L., LL.D. (for Chicago).

F. G. HILTON PRICE, Esq., F.S.A.

MRS. CORNELIUS STEVENSON, SC.D. (for Pennsylvania).

MRS. TIRARD.

THE REV. H. G. TOMKINS, M.A.

EMANUEL M. UNDERDOWN, Esq., Q.C.

SIR HERMANN WEBER, M.D.

E. TOWRY WHYTE, Esq., F.S.A.

MAJOR-GENERAL SIR CHARLES W. WILSON, K.C.B., K.C.M.G., F.R.S.

74191

CONTENTS.

LIST OF PLATES

(WITH REFERENCES TO THE PAGES ON WHICH THEY ARE DESCRIBED).

—————————

THE MASTABA OF PTAHHETEP AND AKHETHETEP.

PART I.
THE CHAPEL OF PTAHHETEP AND THE HIEROGLYPHS.

CHAPTER I.
THE CHAPEL OF PTAHHETEP.

1. The present volume has a natural connexion with that which precedes it in the series of the Archaeological Survey. It was very desirable that *A Collection of Hieroglyphs*, the types figured in which dated from the Middle and New Kingdoms, should be followed by a study of the earlier forms of the signs. Amongst the splendid tombs of the Old Kingdom in the Memphite necropolis, from which such a collection would naturally be gathered, the choice fell upon the chapel of Ptahhetep, so famous for its fine work, which dates from the Vth Dynasty. This selection was largely determined by the loan to the Survey of an almost perfect set of paper squeezes of the walls of the chapel by the Berlin Museum. For this courteous and generous furtherance of its objects the Society is indebted to the good offices of Professor Erman and Dr. Schaefer. The squeezes are of unsurpassable excellence. They were taken many years ago by Herr Ernst Leben, who lived for a long time in Egypt, and after his death they were presented to the Berlin Museum in 1886.

A secondary motive for turning to this tomb existed in a natural desire to know what further inscriptions, if any, the mastaba might contain; for, notwithstanding the descriptions of the tomb by Mariette and Dümichen (*Photographische Resultate*, p. 16), there was reason to believe that other portions of the building were sculptured.

It was determined, therefore, that the chamber should be re-excavated, and that the series of hieroglyphs, most of which had been copied from the squeezes, should be revised on the spot; while at the same time a survey of the mastaba should be made, sufficiently complete to show the relation of the chamber to the rest of the building, and to determine whether there were other sculptured work in the tomb. Any such new material would, of course, be copied in full. In this way the existing publications of an interesting mastaba would be usefully supplemented.

B

2. Accordingly, the necessary permit was asked for and obtained from the Department of Antiquities of Egypt, and I began work at Saqqareh, December 1st, 1898. The excavations soon made it clear that Mariette's summary description of the mastaba (*Voyage*, p. 41), and the plan of it given in his *Mastabas*, p. 359, were equally inadequate and misleading. A T-shaped chamber, of which no hint had ever been given, was found to open out of the central hall on its west side. Further, the whole of this chamber and a part of the corridor of the mastaba were decorated and inscribed in honour of a certain Akhethetep. Yet Mariette's former *reis*, who still survives, certainly excavated the whole tomb, and a reference to this Akhethetep's titles seems to be made by De Rougé (*Les Six Premières Dynasties*, p. 101). In all probability, Akhethetep is to be identified with the similarly named son of Ptahhetep, whose figure appears on the east wall of his father's chapel. No other part of the tomb contains any inscription; the published chapel is, therefore, the only part inscribed for Ptahhetep.

These re-discovered sculptures, added to the hieroglyphs of Ptahhetep's chamber, together with the work of photographing, surveying and the like, afforded me occupation for the whole winter, so that the mastaba was not finally reburied under the sands until May, 1899.

3. The general description of the tomb, and the discussion of all matters relating to Akhethetep, will be reserved for the succeeding memoir. But as a general plan of the mastaba has been included among the plates, in order that the relation of the chapel of Ptahhetep to the other chambers may be seen, a few words must be devoted to it.

The entrance of the mastaba is on the north, and leads into a corridor, which in the direct line has a rather peculiar termination. The visitor passes from it by a doorway on the right into a square hall, the ceiling of which is carried by four pillars. A doorway directly opposite leads from this central hall into the chapel of Akhethetep, while another on the left hand conducts down through a short passage to the chapel of Ptahhetep. The other chambers of the tomb are subsidiary.

It should perhaps be stated, in explanation of the somewhat incomplete state of the plans on Pls. i. and ii., that the excavations necessary for a professionally complete survey of the mastaba, however desirable this might be, were not considered to come within the strict province of the Archaeological Survey, although it was hoped that very useful plans might be constructed without too large an expenditure of time or funds. As will be seen, the mastaba proved to be extensive and of intricate construction. Its outline on two sides is lost in adjoining buildings, and part of it at least was deeply buried. Consequently, although the original proposals were strained to meet the case, it was quite impossible, especially under the conditions of labour at Saqqareh, to undertake the removal of such quantities of material as a complete clearance and reburial of the mastaba would have involved. In addition, the danger of serious damage to the structure, or of accidents to the workmen, obliged me to refrain from excavation in several places. The extent of my clearances can be ascertained from the plans and text, taken in conjunction; so that no unjustified conclusions need be drawn. A detailed explanation of the plans here given and of others will be furnished in the second volume. What they contain will, I venture to hope, prove some atonement for their apparently gratuitous incompleteness in some particulars.

4. The selection of material for this volume has been directed by the intention that it should supplement and complete previous publications as far as possible. The copies of the sculptures made by Miss R. F. E. Paget and Miss A. A. Pirie, and published in Quibell's

Ramesseum by the Egyptian Research Account, with a commentary by Mr. Griffith, have deservedly superseded the plates of Dümichen. The contents of that conscientious piece of work have therefore largely determined those of the present volume. On the one hand, it is hoped that the new material here supplied, and the corrections which the assistance of Mr. Griffith and the better conditions under which I worked have made possible, will give increased value to its predecessor. On the other hand, what the first work contained has only in a very few cases been repeated in this. The desire has been that, while each fulfilled a separate aim, the two together should furnish a complete publication of the chamber of Ptahhetep.

One grave reservation, however, has to be made. This promise is to the student, not to the art-lover. Outline drawings, even the most accurate, are but a poor substitute for the beauty of surfaces in relief; and some of the work in this chamber exhibits that astonishing accuracy, vivacity and freedom which Egyptian art affords when at its oldest and best. We must also picture the chapel as affording, when its glories were fresh, a most brilliant blaze of colour. The bright blue, red, green, and black of the hieroglyphs, the ruddy brown flesh-tints, the yellow animals, and the vivid blue of the water and the wine-vat would be subdued a little, no doubt, by the dull grey of the ground colour. But taken together with the deep red of the ceiling, and the magnificent scheme of variegated colour on the false door, they would have an effect which it is difficult for the imagination to approach. The present condition of the walls is of no great help in the effort. Little catches the eye but the blue-grey background; for though traces of paint are numerous, they are generally very faint and fragmentary indeed.

5. Some attempt has been made in this volume to make good the absence of relief in the plates of the Ramesseum by the inclusion of a series of photographs of the east wall, the scenes of which are not only the most interesting but also the finest in execution, together with a few pictures of the west and north walls. These photographs, while doing but faint justice to the work, will at least afford some idea of its character. (A good photograph of the *fracas* among the boatmen, from the east wall, had been previously published by Mariette in his *Voyage dans la Haute Égypte*, but is accessible there to very few.)

To meet the second deficiency in some degree, a reproduction in colour of the patterns employed on the ornamented false door has been included. The fragments of paint still left were sufficient to make the restoration almost, if not quite, complete. The signification of this door and the character of its decoration being both of great interest, and no doubt intimately connected with one another, it seemed advisable to add these plates to the volume, although an elaborate copy had previously been published in Perrot and Chipiez's *Histoire de l'Art*. A comparison of those plates with the original showed that the draughtsman, M. Bourgoin, had followed the original with extreme accuracy. My copy will be found to differ very little from his. Indeed, I am indebted to it for confirmation of my own notes in one or two particulars where these proved not to have been sufficiently explicit.

Further, the reader has often much difficulty in obtaining from a series of plates or photographs any idea of the whole scene as it presents itself to an eye-witness. A key-plate of the east wall has therefore been provided in Pl. xxi., the main part of which is derived by permission from the plates of the E. R. A. volume. This, with the photographs and the plans in Pl. ii., will, it is hoped, materially aid the reader in picturing to himself the chamber as it exists.

The love of the Egyptian people for animal

B 2

life gave the artists among them a specially keen eye for this subject, and peculiar freedom in the treatment of it. The exception which has been made in favour of some of the animals on the east wall in Pl. xxii. will therefore need no other justification.

6. As will be seen from the plans, the chapel of Ptahhetep is the inmost room of the mastaba, and is reached through the corridor and pillared hall, and lastly through a passage or ante-room, which is furnished with a shelved recess on the west side. The floor of the chapel is on a lower level than that of the corridor, and, to judge from the position of the doorsill, than that of the great hall also. The ceiling also of this chamber is nearly two feet lower than that of the hall. The room measures 17 feet 5 inches by 7 feet 2 inches, the greatest length being north and south. It is 12 feet 4 inches in height; 9 feet of this is sculptured, and is of fine white limestone, while the lower courses are of coarser stone. It is very massively constructed. The west wall, which contains the two false doors and measures about 200 square feet, is formed by two enormous blocks, each of which occupies half the space. They are naturally of immense thickness also. To obtain the projection of the torus moulding and the cavetto cornice of the southern door, the whole remaining surface of the huge stone must have been reduced by several inches. The pride which this ancient people took in feats of mechanical enterprise seems to have led them to consider that an erection, or any part of it, was most noble in proportion as it approached construction in a single piece. In this case the extreme of massive simplicity was only given to the wall that held the sacred doors. The other walls, though containing some very large blocks, do not exhibit equal ambition. They are built up of several stones, and in places some very small pieces are used. It is as a consequence of this patching that the east wall has suffered its only serious mutilation.

7. The ceiling is formed of two immense roofing stones, the under surface of which is coloured a warm red, and is grooved to represent a roofing formed by the trunks of palm-trees laid transversely across the chamber. A section of the stone is given in Pl. ii. From this it will be seen that the imitation is no longer realistic, unless it be the trimmed baulks which are here represented. A somewhat similar ceiling is to be seen in a rock-hewn tomb in the necropolis of Gizeh. The northernmost roofing-stone is broken completely across in a way to cause great apprehension to all who hope that this fine example of an Old Kingdom funerary chapel may be preserved in its present state for many generations to come. The danger is not lessened by the great mound of sand which is heaped above it with the commendable intention of preserving the chamber from violation.

8. The east wall is disfigured by an oblong hole which has been made through the sculptures at the centre (see Pl. xxi.). Except at the face of the wall it is perfectly regular in shape. I owe to Professor Petrie a satisfactory solution of this puzzle. It would seem that a slip of stone of this size was used by the original builders to repair some irregularity in the upper surface of a large block. This neat insertion proved too tempting to plunderers, who prised it out for building-stone. A gap in the list of offerings on the west wall seems due to the same temptation and offence.

An attempt has also been made upon the upper part of the south wall, but the block seems to have proved too massive for the violators. A hole, however, has been forced near the ceiling, and the sculptures have been injured at the joint of the masonry by the concussion from the blows. Slight injuries, due apparently to natural causes, are observable also in a few places on the east and north walls. The photographs reveal in addition how wantonly the walls, particularly on the east and south, have been defaced by blows from a mattock, or similar instrument, perhaps in an attempt to locate suspected chambers behind. But it must also be confessed that the processes of wet-squeezing and cast-taking, which were in vogue in former days, have probably been responsible for some injury to the sculptures, and certainly for a lamentable removal of colour. Happily now there is a universal desire to preserve intact for the future what the past has bequeathed, and an increasing provision by the authorities of the necessary means to realise this desire.

9. The east and south walls are pierced just below the ceiling by a shallow longitudinal opening, both wall and roof being cut away to form the shaft, which slants down into the chamber, presumably from the open air above. As the openings are at present blocked up and deeply buried, their further direction towards the outside of the mastaba could not be investigated. They were evidently designed to admit light or air, perhaps both. I do not know whether such apertures frequently occur in mastabas. Something similar exists in the pillared hall also, and I have observed the like in the hall of a mastaba in the necropolis of Gizeh. The manner of this construction can be seen in Pl. ii.

10. In the hope of recovering some of the fragments from the broken walls I caused the chamber to be cleared down to the original floor level, where I found the greater part of a stone pavement remaining. In front of the inscribed false door a simple table of offerings was found, and its position, as well as the way in which it lay embedded in a thin layer of mud, seemed to prove conclusively that it was the original and *in situ*. It is of a somewhat rough and yellowish stone, and bears no signs of having been inscribed. For its position and its form consult Pls. i. and ii. The only other object found was the lid of a sarcophagus, hewn out of white limestone, which lay a few inches

from the east wall near its centre. A chamfer has been roughly cut along the upper edge of the two sides: the under side is flat, and the stone bears no inscription. It evidently is a relic of one of the many later burials for which the tomb has been put to use. The drawing on Pl. ii. was made afterwards from measurements, and is much too regular in outline.

Though disappointed here, I nevertheless had the pleasure of repairing in a small degree the injuries which the sculptures have sustained. A fragment which the workmen brought from the excavations outside the south wall of the mastaba, just behind this chamber, proved to belong to the scenes of the east wall. Accordingly I instituted a careful search, and was rewarded by the discovery of several other fragments, which I was able to fit into their places, and which, as luck would have it, made good the greater part of a tantalizing lacuna in the titles of Ptahhetep on the south wall (see Pl. iii.). Another fragment belonged to a missing nome-sign on the same wall (see Pl. xvi.). It seems likely, therefore, that at the time of Mariette's discovery all the chips from the broken surfaces lay on the floor of the chamber, and might have been preserved. Further sifting of the *débris* outside the south wall would probably recover many more of them. The above-mentioned fragments I fixed in their places with cement: a few others I buried in a tin in the south-east corner of the chamber.

11. The scenes, and still more the hieroglyphs, of the chamber differ considerably in the quality of their execution. Those on the east wall are in very bold relief and carefully executed, though it must not be taken for granted that the finish and attention to detail is uniform even in closely proximate parts. The scenes on the upper portions of the north and south walls are much worn, and those in the thickness of the doorway seem to have been of poor execution from the first. This variableness in the work frequently coincides with a

similar difference in the quality of the stone, and is doubtless largely due to it. The acme of excellence is reached in the charming hieroglyph fig. 69. In the case of the first and last of the animals in the upper row of Pl. xxii. the inner lines seem to be outlines which have been abandoned, though in the former case these lines seem to be really the more correct. The amount of painted detail in the chamber which was not utilised by the sculptor, or was added to his work afterwards, is considerable. Probably such details were often intentionally left uncut, either as being too minute or in order that the scene might not become confused; but in other cases carelessness or haste seems to have prevented completion. Signs are not wanting that the draughtsman laid down his designs not only in outline, but, roughly at least, in colour also; partly perhaps as an additional guide to the sculptor, partly to satisfy himself as to the general scheme. Here and there, as often happens in other tombs, names and titles of servitors are but roughly cut out or incised, or else are indicated only in colour (ink?). Of these survivals in paint the most important are the two nome-signs on the south wall, which have been read with fair certainty. Very interesting too are the painted bushes in the desert scene (Pl. xxii.). They are now much obliterated, and appear to have been too conventional in colour and outline to aid much in the identification of the ancient flora.[1] The gap in the upper register

on the extreme left hand seems to have been occupied by a painted tree.

It may be worthy of mention here that two of the most characteristic scenes in the chamber, the games of the boys and the animals in the desert, are paralleled very closely in the tomb of Mera near by, one of the three mastabas in this great necropolis which are open to the public. Most of the sculpture there cannot be compared for workmanship with that in Ptahhetep's chapel, showing the decline of art in two or three generations. Ptahhetep's tomb was decorated during the reign of Assa in the Vth Dynasty, and Mera's during the reigns of Teta and Pepy I. of the VIth Dynasty.

12. A word remains to be said concerning the decoration of the false doors.

NORTH FALSE DOOR.—In Pl. xix. a representation of this door has been given, from which the whole scheme of colour may be made out with the help of the following notes. (The painted designs on the left side, being a repetition of those on the right, have been omitted in this plate in order that the parts which sculpture and colour play in the decoration may be more clearly distinguished. Cf. also the photograph, Pl. xxix.). All the patterns which fill the panels will be found in the coloured plates xx. and xxA., and can be identified by help of the letters employed. The horizontal bands, the decoration of which is not indicated, are simply coloured red. The topmost horizontal panel has a ribbed surface, and is painted green. Where the door may be considered to be unornamented (back and sides of the vertical grooves, background of the draught-board pattern, &c.), a light yellow has been employed. The deep recess beneath the round lintel is painted and grained to represent a door made up of very narrow planks of wood, and turning on metal (?) pivots. Sockets of such pivots seem to be indicated by black angle-pieces, which are seen at the top and bottom right-hand corners of the grained recess, both of

[1] Those who do not know the Egyptian desert, or who are only familiar with the barren wastes further south, may wonder at the application of the term "desert" to ground containing so much plant life. But the dews and winter rains, which fall in fair quantity in the vicinity of Saqqareh, enable a varied vegetation to grow in the hollows, especially one succulent variety, which, if some license be granted to the ancient artist, may be recognized amongst those which he has pourtrayed on this wall. In the early part of the year the flocks of goats and sheep are driven by herd-girls to browse on this produce of the desert, and the visitor may gather a nosegay of varied and interesting flowers.

this and the south false door. It is uncertain whether the lintel also was grained.

The decoration is terminated below by two deep horizontal bands of red and of yellow, each bordered above with black. The "cord" pattern, which Professor Petrie has now carried back to the Ist Dynasty, also ends here. (In Pl. xix. it is extended incorrectly to the bottom of the groove.) A strip, extending completely across the right half of the door near the foot, is reproduced in Pl. xx., and exhibits not only the five patterns employed on the door-jambs, but also an interesting representation from which it would appear that long pieces of matting or similar material were wont to be laid over the blank spaces of the walls on either side of important doorways, and laced down taut to loops fixed below.

SOUTH FALSE DOOR (see Pl. xxix.).—This door is chiefly decorated, as the walls are, by painted hieroglyphs and figures in relief on a dull grey background. Scarcely any of the colouring now remains. The door is further ornamented in the customary way by a torus moulding and "cavetto" cornice, the latter painted with vertical bands of colour, slightly separated from one another, in the order blue, green, red, green. The recess is treated like that of the north false door, but without division into planks. The drum is coloured red. Traces of paint in the recesses on either side of the tablet show that they were occupied by a miniature representation resembling the north door, with all the detail which the space allowed.

13. The colours on Pl. xviii. have been reproduced as closely as possible from the fragments of paint which remain. Where there was no guide to the colour the space has been left blank (border of huntsman's dress; apex of pyramid, fig. 400; bands at the foot of the tower, fig. 406; hair riband (?), fig. 398, &c.).

CHAPTER II.

THE SCULPTURED SCENES IN PTAHHETEP'S CHAPEL.

BY THE EDITOR.

THE sculptures of the chamber of Ptahhetep have already been described by the present writer, from the complete outline tracings of Miss Pirie and Miss Paget, in a volume of the Egyptian Research Account entitled *The Ramesseum* (by J. E. Quibell), *and the Tomb of Ptahhetep.* He need not therefore deal at length with the history of their discovery and publication a second time before entering more particularly upon the subjects of the plates of the present volume.

The small rectangular chamber is entered from the N., and from about 3 feet above the ground the whole of the interior walls and the thickness of the walls in the doorway are adorned with sculpture, once brilliantly coloured. The ceiling is carved in imitation of a timber roofing.

The sculptures are not without a certain sequence in their arrangement upon the walls. They put on record the name, titles, occupations and surroundings of the man in his lifetime and his provision for services after death, apparently with a view not only to the honour of his memory among men, but also to a corresponding reception and perfect welfare for him amongst the gods. Those of the W. wall in particular—the false doors and the ritual scenes —cannot have been intended merely to record the presentation of the funeral offerings by the priests; their presence in the tomb was designed to produce a magic influence upon the dead man's future, providing him mystically with a permanent equipment for the endless repetition of the services figured. Such has

long been the view of Maspero, and it is now generally accepted.

In the passage of the doorway servants are represented bringing into the chamber offerings of flesh and fowl.[1] Similar scenes are continued on to the W. wall. On entering the chamber first we pass a scene of slaughter on the lower half of the front or N. wall (Pl. xxx.*b*); then, on the W. wall a false door (p. 6), highly decorated but without inscription (Pls. xix., xx., xxix.*a*), beyond which is figured the scene of the table of offerings, or grand ceremonial meal of the deceased—the list of the offerings is shown on Pl. xxx.*a*. Beyond this is another false door, fully inscribed for Ptahhetep and sculptured with a brief *résumé* of a similar meal (Pl. xxix.*b*). Again, at the inner end of the chamber, the S. wall shows Ptahhetep's meal, with servants and priests slaughtering cattle and bringing food, while abundant supplies are brought by figures in the upper rows which symbolize the estates of Ptahhetep.[2] That each of these banquets is ceremonial and funerary is suggested by the fact that priests are always figured as present. But it is possible that the scene on the inner wall represents the supplies and food of Ptahhetep in his lifetime, since here the priests are not conspicuous: perhaps they were there only to bless the food? This scene then may belong to the series relating to the life of Ptahhetep.

It is to this series that the most interesting

---

[1] *Ram.*, Pl. xxxvii.
[2] *Ram.*, Pls. xxxiv., xxxv., top.

and beautiful of the scenes belong, which are also less conventional than the representation of ceremonies of offering. The uninscribed false door on the W. wall may be intended as their starting-point, and to represent the façade of Ptahhetep's house; but this is very uncertain. On the N. wall, above the level of the entrance (Pl. xxx.*b*), we have a scene of the morning and indoor occupations of Ptahhetep; and two outdoor scenes occupy the whole of the E. wall (general outline, Pl. xxi.; for the details see Frontispiece and Pls. xxiii.-xxviii.). The first of these latter figures the amusements and occupations of the people in the desert and the marshes viewed by Ptahhetep, who has gone out afield towards mid-day (?) in undress costume. In the other of these scenes the great man is in more official garb. Perhaps the time is towards evening, when the hunters are bringing home their spoil; the farmyards also are being inspected, and their contributions of cattle and birds are brought in. Then we may suppose that the meal, with the varied contributions to it figured on the S. wall, represents the evening meal in the house itself. It is impossible to give a perfectly consistent account of these scenes in a few words, for the artist put so much into each of them as to cause overlaps. Some omissions, notwithstanding, are very noticeable. Agriculture, the most characteristic of Egyptian employments, is here entirely unrepresented, though ploughing and sowing are commonly figured in the tombs of the Old Kingdom. So also with arts and crafts of all kinds. Probably we may trace some personal predilections of Ptahhetep in the choice of subjects.

On Pl. xxx.*b* we see to the left of the entrance four rows [1] of men bringing offerings—as it were to the Grand False Door—and slaughtering cattle. Above the level of the door is a separate scene of the morning occupations of Ptahhetep, who is reading and hearing reports during the progress of his toilet.[2] Three hounds and a favourite monkey are sitting beneath his chair, while attendants are busy with his feet and coiffure.

It is the E. wall, however, which displays the best workmanship of the tomb, and of this a very good idea is given by a succession of photographs on Pls. xxiii.-xxviii.[3] In the first scene the great man, having cast off his wig and his false beard (see Frontispiece), is "looking at every good pastime that is done in the whole land." It was the practice and pleasure of the grandees to walk or be carried about inspecting the work of the fields, and most of the out-of-doors occupations here figured (Pls. xxiii., xxv., xxvi.) are particularly joyous and picturesque.

In the top row (see Pl. xxiii.) we have papyrus-gathering in the marshes, and the leading of cattle across a pool where crocodiles lie in wait for stragglers. Mr. Davies has here made an interesting addition (in Pl. iii.) to the cattle-scene as formerly published, and now we see clearly the herdsmen in the boat. One punts, another is guiding a calf by a cord, and they are exclaiming at the crocodile, "O filthy one, may your heart be pleased with the water-weeds (?)."[4]

In the second row boys are playing games, and from the names of the games we may conclude that a vintage festival is here represented, the vintage scene itself being in the next row. The first game is throwing pointed sticks at the ground, "Throwing darts for (?) Shesemu,"[5] Shesemu being perhaps the vintage god. Then come two boys

[1] Cf. *Ram.*, Pl. xxxvi.

[2] *Ib.*, Pl. xxxv., lower half.
[3] See also *Ram.*, Pls. xxxi.-xxxiii.
[4] Cf. *Mast. de Mera*, p. 526, for the name of the weed, and MASP., *Ét. Ég.*, ii., p. 110, for a variant of this curious inscription.
[5] Cf. *Mast. de Mera*, p. 564, for *stt n.*

seated on the ground holding their feet in their hands; and below them a boy is carrying on his back two small children, who by holding each other's legs form as it were panniers on each side of him: he is evidently playing donkey. Behind these, two boys are standing together, each with an arm round the other's neck, and holding the arm of his fellow with the other hand; they appear to be going in opposite directions, and each, perhaps, is endeavouring to free his own arm and get the other's head in chancery. The inscription is very doubtful: "Two nurslings overturned (?)." Next is a youth wearing a kind of shoulder scarf, who is striding towards two lads sitting on the ground, each of whom has the heel of one foot resting on the toes of the other below, his hands placed also one above the other, and with fingers extended. The accompanying inscription seems to read, "Thirst that is in the ground." Next we have a boy on all-fours upon the shoulders of three of his companions; to this probably belongs the inscription "Setting the vine-trellis." Behind this group six boys appear to have formed a ring, and then, putting their feet together and falling back at full stretch to be making a revolving circle on their heels: the inscription says, "Go round four times." In the last group, a boy, kneeling on the ground, is trying to catch the feet of his four companions, who confuse him by simultaneous attacks on all sides. The inscription may be read, "Behold you have kicked me!" or perhaps, "Let me strike at you!" "I am weary in my sides," and "I have tasted (?) you."

In the third row men are watering a vine, plucking and trampling the grapes, squeezing out the juice.

The fourth row (see Pls. xxv.-xxvi.) shows a fine scene of hunting in the desert, and traces still remain of the painted herbage, &c. Compare the careful outlines of this row in Pl. xxii.*b.* In the upper division a Nubian greyhound

(*slughi*) attacks two wild hyenas or hyena dogs, another worries an oryx, a gazelle suckles her fawn, a *slughi* catches an ibex, and there are two leopards and two jackals. In the lower division two *slughis* are held in leash by a huntsman who is wrapped in a brilliantly coloured garment (figured in Pl. xviii.); a small dog of peculiar type is in front of him. He points to a wild (?) bull attacked by a lion, which has seized its muzzle to its great distress. A *slughi* rolls over a gazelle, another pulls down an oryx; there are also a bubale and two wild bulls, of which one is captured by a man with a bola or lasso which has wound itself round the horns and body. Above these, in the background, a gazelle lies under a bush, an ichneumon is hunting in the herbage, a jerboa is taking refuge in a hillock, one of two hedgehogs has captured a grasshopper. The plants, as usual, are quite unrecognizable in the quaintly simplified rendering of the ancient artist.

The fifth row represents scenes on the river bank.—Splitting fish to dry in the sun; the bladders are taken out and lie on the ground. An old man and a boy are "twisting ropes of boat-building," as the inscription says. A man says to a boy, "O strong youth (*S'qy*, cf. Arabic *yâ gedaʿ*), bring me ropes"; the boy replies, "O my father, here is the rope for you," offering him two coils.

The sixth row is a scene of fowling with clap-nets. A man stands up to give the signal crying, "Pull comrades, there is a catch for you." Where the birds are put in boxes or cages the inscription is, "Put these in this box."

In the seventh row we have a mock combat between the crews of three boats. In the third boat an aged man is enjoying a comfortable meal; evidently he is one favoured of the master. He is entitled, "his beloved and trusty *mehenk*, the chief sculptor Ankhenptah." Here then we have the name (though hardly the features) of the really great artist who executed these sculptures, signed in the corner of his masterpiece.

The second scene on the E. wall is given in Pls. xxi. (right half), xxiv., xxvii., xxviii. It shows Ptahhetep with his usual long wig and false beard "seeing the gifts and contributions of the villages of the North and South." In the top row (Pl. xxiv.) there is wrestling by the trained youths, a body of whom are also marching up a prisoner they have captured, perhaps only as a military exercise. In the next two rows is the return of the huntsmen with their spoil. The robed huntsman leads his *slughis*, and the small dog follows at his heels: the captured hyena-dogs (?) also are held by a leash. A man carries by a yoke two cages containing hares and hedgehogs; another carries trophies of the chase, including antelope and ibex skins in a bundle. A lion and a leopard, each in a strong wooden cage, are drawn along on sledges; below an oryx, an ibex, an addax, and a bubale are being led. These are typical of the larger kind of game; hence we may conclude that the elegant and peculiar antelope behind them belongs to some large species (Soemmering's?). The figure is unique in our knowledge. (Pl. xxii. *a.*)

The remainder of this scene (Pls. xxvii., xxviii.) concerns the farmyard strictly. In the fifth row cattle are being fed artificially, a cow is calving; calves are tethered above : cattle "of the Thoth festival"—which was held at the beginning of the New Year, i.e. in July— are brought up. In the sixth row two fat oxen are being led forward for inspection, one long-horned with a shell hanging from its neck, the other short-horned; for the shell see Pl. xvi., "Miscellaneous Details," top left. In the seventh row is a fine series of domesticated birds, in groups, with numbers written beside them: cranes (*zat*); *re*-geese 121,200; *terp*-geese 121,200; Egyptian geese (*hep* or *smen*) —not a very good kind—11,110; swan (unique representation in Egyptian art) 1225; pin-tailed duck 120,000 ; widgeon 121,022 ; pigeons 111,200. The last group of birds has no numerals attached to it. Previously I had conjectured them to be quails or partridges,[1] but from the photograph and from a beautiful cast sent me by the authorities of the Berlin Museum, they seem rather to resemble young geese. If so, they may be meant to indicate the innumerable young of Ptahhetep's poultry yard, the goose being taken as the typical domestic fowl; it would thus be implied that in the vast numbers of fowl recorded only grown birds are counted.

_____

Ram., p. 30.

CHAPTER III.

THE HIEROGLYPHS OF PTAHHETEP AND AKHETHETEP.

By the Editor.

N.B.—*Throughout this chapter, the scenes and inscriptions from Ptahhetep's chamber in which the hieroglyphs occur are generally referred to as shown in the plates of "The Ramesseum." Plate-numbers up to XXX. refer to the present volume, and those from XXXI. to XLI. to "The Ramesseum." For abbreviations see "Hieroglyphs," p. ix.; for transliteration, ib. pp. x., xi. An asterisk (*) marks a hieroglyphic type as inexact.*

Those who may be working upon the history of Egyptian writing will be glad to have references to reviews of the volume on *Hieroglyphs*, which formed the sixth memoir of the Archaeological Survey. It has been reviewed by Maspero in the *Revue Critique*, October, 1899, p. 261; by W. Max Müller in *Orientalischer Literaturzeitung*, 1899, p. 266 (cf. a special article on the non-acrophonic origin of the hieroglyphic alphabet, *id. ib.* p. 259); and by Piehl, *Sphinx*, iii., p. 46. Professor Maspero's review is very suggestive, and of especial value as treating individually twenty-three separate hieroglyphs; Max Müller's deals rather with general principles or with questions of pure philology. Each writer corrects indubitable errors in *Hieroglyphs*, and each appears to me to uphold one or more untenable theories. If little use has been made of these reviews—so full of valuable information and suggestions—in the preparation of this chapter, it is because most of the material for it was collected before they appeared, and also because one cannot, with each instalment of facsimiles and notes, give space for full discussion of details and of disputed points. This must be left to some future time, when the progress of knowledge and an accumulation of examples may have

made possible a final settlement of the origin of most of the signs and of their values.

There must also be noted as of great importance for Egyptian phonology and for the values of signs, the first volume of Sethe's elaborate and very original study on the Egyptian verb. It is from time to time referred to in the following pages. Sethe's main view in regard to the writing is that it is purely consonantal, and that weak letters, which in many words were etymologically appropriate but had lost their phonetic value, were from early times introduced inappropriately into other words by false analogy.

We here publish a nearly complete set of types of hieroglyphs from the sculptured chambers of Ptahhetep and Akhethetep. Their value as specimens is naturally very unequal. In discussing varieties of signs care is always required to discriminate between unfinished or injured examples and genuine new forms. The scenes and inscriptions in this mastaba were carefully sketched in inks for the sculptor to work on. In the chambers of Akhethetep considerable wall-spaces so prepared were left entirely untouched by the chisel; in other places the sculptor has done his work imper-

·fectly, and even where he completed it there is, as elsewhere, great inequality in the finish. One example of a sign is left with a plain surface, while in another instance—perhaps only a few inches away—it is crowded with elaborate detail not essential to the sign, but of great aid to the investigator in determining its pictorial significance. The beautiful example of ♦, fig. 296, is an instance of such welcome but unnecessary elaboration in contrast with its surroundings. On the other hand, in some cases distinctive characteristics are omitted even where the omission may lead to doubt or confusion; thus ▥ and ▦ may be left plain and indistinguishable from ▭. Elsewhere the sculptor, either in sinking the ground or in carving the sign itself, may have mistakenly cut away what he should have left in relief: in one case in Ptahhetep (xxxiv., col. 2) the points of ▱ have been carelessly removed, leaving only ▭. There are cases in which the designer has omitted or the mason has smoothed out whole signs, which were afterwards roughly chiselled in or painted. Add to all these considerations that some walls are much more carefully sculptured than others, and it is obvious that although the tomb of Ptahhetep is acknowledged to be one of the very finest known in the necropolis of Saqqareh, this fact does not guarantee the perfection of every hieroglyph in its inscriptions. These contain some very rare and interesting signs—especially those of the nomes—and some peculiarly fine examples of common ones, and it is well worth while to study the forms and uses of the hieroglyphs throughout pretty exhaustively. This I have done far more comfortably than and almost as completely as if the originals had been before me, by means of the Berlin squeezes and Mr. Davies' photographs and hand copies of details from the chamber of Ptahhetep, and his drawn copies of the whole of the sculptures from the chambers of Akhethetep. The chief drawback lay in the absence from this material of the faint traces of colour remaining on the original; but even with regard to this Mr. Davies had throughout made very careful notes. Had the original colours been fully preserved, the value of the tomb for our purposes would have been immensely greater.

In Mr. Davies' figures, though little attempt has been made to reproduce the artistic effect of the reliefs, the utmost care has been taken to render the lines of the sculptures with absolute fidelity.

Class I. Human Figures. Pl. IV.

🐣 (*Hier.*, p. 11); child as seated on its nurse's knee, sucking its finger, no lock of hair (so also *Medum*, Pl. ix.), *Pth.*, xxxvi. 3, xxxvii. 2 (**fig. 12**); *Akht.* (**fig. 16**). Here word-sign with final ♦ in proper name for ◄ ♦ "child" (*Dend.*, Pl. vii.). Elsewhere det. of childhood and youth: note especially its use in military matters, of recruits and trained youth—*nfr, z'm.*

Sitting figures:—

🐣 (*Hier.*, p. 11); **fig. 6**, *Akht.*, bearded; in *Pth.*, xxxii. 2, xxxiv. 3, xxxix., left, 4, &c., beardless. This and many other signs illustrate the ordinary sitting posture of the old Egyptians as represented in their paintings and sculptures; it is a kind of combination of sitting and kneeling, one knee being raised, the other on the ground, and the buttock resting on the heel. Here det. of man (not for proper names). Elsewhere in O.K. = *s*, "man": L., *D.*, ii., 43*d*, 2 *ad fin.*; *Dend.*, Pl. xxxvii.c, l. 570, heading.

🐣 man seated with one hand raised, the other to the ground. The speaking man with palm outwards, *Pth.*, iii. top, xxxii. 2 (**fig. 4**), xxxiii. 1, &c. (det. of exclamation), is distinguished from the eating man with hand to mouth, *Pth.*, xxxi., top (imperfect—see "Corrections," p. 42), xli. 3 (**fig. 18**); *Akht.* (**fig. 25**). Word-sign for *wnm*, "eat," and det. of eating. The first form is elsewhere det. of speech, and sometimes probably word-sign for the exclamation 𓇌 "O!" The two signs were probably confused early, as concerning actions of the mouth.

𓀢 seated man, both hands upraised before the face : *Pth.*, xxxiii. top (**fig. 7**); cf. fig. 23. Det. of *śm'*, "stranger" (?); cf. *Pyr. N.* 586, *Rec. de Trav.*, xv., 178, l. 4, temp. Thothmes IV. In *Trois Années*, 187, it is even employed as word-sign for *śm'* in a proper name. Indicates supplication (?), begging, beggarly persons, &c.: cf. *tw', św'* det. with this sign; also *dw'* (*Pyr. T.* 242), *y'w*, "praise."

𓀠 bearded man—priest—with arms raised in adoration, det. of *w'b* written with the sign of water—blue in *Pth.*—pouring from a vase (*Hier.*, p. 40), the two signs forming the fixed compound group for *w'b*, "priest": *Pth.*, xxxiii., col. 8 (**fig. 23**), &c.

𓀾 seated man, one hand steadying basket on head, the other on ground as if he were about to rise : bearded in *Akht.* (**fig. 5**). Word-sign for *k''t*, "work"; elsewhere det. of and sometimes word-sign for *f'*, "carry" (*Bul. Pap.*, no. xviii., &c.). In O.K. *f'*, "carry," is often expressed by the man supporting 𓈖 on his head; beardless in *Pth.*, xli. 1 (**fig. 9**), see also *Mera*, p. 529.

Besides the above there are two uncommon seated figure signs. (1) Holding *sekhem* sceptre and curved staff resembling that in 𓋤 : *Pth.*, xli. 21 (**fig. 8**)—a rare word-sign for *ḥnmś* 𓏤 〰 𓀾 𓏤 (cf. *Peduamenap*, Pl. xxi., no. 49), which seems to mean "respected friend" or "companion," "to be friendly." (In *L.*, *D.*, ii., 67, it occurs again, but without the staff, and in early M.K. it is sometimes replaced by 𓀻,

L., *D.*, ii., 145*a*, 147*a*.) (2) The *kher-heb*, or lector, bearded, holding a roll and with a band across the breast and over the shoulder: *Pth.*, xxxix., left, 4 (**fig. 2**). For the remarkable figure of a man holding filth (?) on Pl. iii., top, see below, p. 36 (fig. 385).

Upright figures :—

(1) The beater, wearing a slight workman's loin-cloth, combined with 𓏃—coloured green—in *Pth.*, xxxiii. 5 (**fig. 1**): also *Akht.* Word-sign for *ḥ*, *ḥw*, "strike." Especially after O.K., the beater is a common det. of violent action = 𓌕 (*Hier.*, p. 15). After O.K. the present compound was disused in hieroglyphic, and in hieratic it was misinterpreted as 𓀻.

(2) Eager workman, beardless, running forward with hands clenched, apparently to undertake work, wearing the same loin-cloth as (1): *Pth.*, xxxix., right, 3 (**fig. 15**), and left, 4. Word-sign for 𓇋 𓈖 "by," as a particle expressing more or less emphatically the connexion of the agent with the action of the verb in a sentence.

(3) 𓀻. Aged man walking, leaning on a staff forked below. In **fig. 14**, *Pth.*, xxxii., over the son, the breast is pendant, so also markedly in **fig. 21**, xxxix., left, 1; *ib.* xxxix., right, 4, the head is bald in front but the breast normal, in *Akht.* (stele) hair (red) and breast are both normal. The values of this sign are numerous and difficult to fix. In titles, as subst. preceding *h'y't*, &c., 𓀻 = *śmśw*; cf. *Pap. Hood*, no. 67 (Br., *Aegypt.*, p. 218), and *śmśw......t*, *Pyr. T.* 87 = *N.* 618. But as adj. 𓀻 generally = *wr*, though in the title of the mourners 𓀻 𓂝 probably is 𓂝 𓃀 𓂝 (*Paheri*, Pl. v.), and in *L.*, *D.*, ii., 113*b*, it stands for both '' and *wr* in a single well-known formula. 𓀻 = *śr*, "a noble," with rad. ext., and sometimes *wr*, "a chief." 𓇌𓀻, 𓀻 = 𓇋 𓃀 𓂝 "old age" (*Kah. Pap.*, p. 30); but in the tomb formula 𓀻𓏤 of *Pth.*, xxxix. varies with 𓀻 𓈖 𓇌 𓏤 *śmśy* (?) *nfr* in *Deud.*, v.A., cf. *ib.*, vi. In offerings 𓀻 𓏤 = *ḥnmś*, *Peduamenap*, xxiv., no. 92. Det. of old

age, position of elder, &c.; det. also, occasionally of *tw'*, "beggar," &c. How far the distinction in form apparently made in some texts between the bowed old man and the noble is to be carried through is doubtful; in these tombs there is no clear sign of such distinction. In L., D., ii., 149e, l. 9, 🐦 may stand for 𓂝 "quarryman." For *śmśy* (?) *nfr* cf. SETHE, *Verbum*, i., p. 257.

The only *kneeling* sign; **fig. 17**, *Pth.*, xli. 1: man, bearded, with hands on an oval mass of earth (?) (coloured blue in xli. 15, where it wrongly (?) follows *sf*), over which water is being poured from a vase. Word-sign for "wash the table (?)," and *st*, "foundation stone." The man may be kneading clay.

(*Hier.*, p. 13); watchman with staff: **fig. 10**, *Pth.*, xxxi. 1, beardless, and plain staff; **fig. 19**, *Akht.*, bearded, and ? on stick. Word-sign for *s'w*, "herdsman": in NEWBERRY, *Rekhm.*, ii., 6, 17, the figures *yri* and *s'w* are identical. **Fig. 20**, *Pth.*, xxxiv. 1, woman fully robed, apparently with fillet round head and tied at back (see the same place-name, MAR., *Mast.*, 353; L., D., ii., 46—*Pehenuka*) and holding stick crossed by ?, must be the female guardian. Word-sign for *yr·t*.

seated man, fully robed, with long wig and long beard slightly curved forward and generally knobbed at end: **fig. 3**, *Pth.*, xxxviii., col. 2—with lappet on shoulder by exception, all other examples without this lappet; **fig. 11**, *Akht.* Probably represents obsolete costume of the "ancestors." Corresponds as det. (and suffix) for "god" to 🐒 as det. (and suffix) for "man" (*Hier.*, p. 11); but as word-sign for "god," as in = *ntr* ⁽ᵒ⁾, *Pth.*, xxxviii. *l.c.*, it is rare. In *Pth.*, xxxviii. 1 and xxxix., left, 4, accompanied by or compounded with 𓊽 alone it stands for "Osiris."

man fully robed and bearded, seated on stool with usual animal legs: **fig. 24**, *Akht.*—rough example. Word-sign for *śpś*, "venerable," "precious," as first clearly proved by MASP., *Ä. Z.*, 1882, 130. Fig. 147 in *Hier.* (p. 13), used as det. of names &c. of venerable people, is the same sign; cf. also *Medum*, Pl. xxiv.

goddess Maat, represented standing with close-fitting dress suspended from the shoulders, large wig with fillet and ostrich feather (*Hier.*, p. 23), holding (*Hier.*, p. 59) and (*Hier.*, p. 60): **fig. 13**, *Pth.*, xxxix., right, 2; **fig. 398** (coloured), *Akht.* After O.K. generally seated figure. Word-sign for the name of the goddess. It is remarkable that in *Pyr.* her name is determined by a hawk (?) wearing the feather on its head.

the god of Busiris on the sacred perch (*Hier.*, p. 58): **fig. 22**, *Pth.*, xxxiv. top. This much injured sign seems at present unique for O.K. (faint and doubtful in the corrections on p. 42), though there are abbreviated forms of it in *Pyr.*, where in M. 199, N. 543, according to published texts, the figure holds ⌐ and ∧, and wears double plumes; in N. 717 the head is bare and | is substituted for ⌐. In the Berlin squeeze little more can be discerned than in Mr. Davies' drawing. The headdress cannot be feathers, and is evidently ⌐ (cf. *Hier.*, p. 60), thus agreeing with the instance in MAR., *Ab.*, i., p. 78. The figure seems to have been represented leaning slightly forward on his staff. The end of his divine beard is seen as resting on his arm. In later inscriptions the god wears two feathers as a headdress, often accompanied by ram's horns, and this figure is the favourite det. of the word *yty*, "reigning (?) king"; cf. *Hier.*, p. 13, fig. 161. Probably he represents the living Eastern Osiris (v. *Pyr.*, *l.c.*, T. 146, &c.) as opposed to the dead "Chief of the Westerners at Abydos." See *P. S. B. A.*,

1899, p. 278. Word-sign for ⌐⌐⌐ ʿnzˑt, the name of the Busirite nome, the IXth of Lower Egypt, *Pyr. N.* 717 = *W.* 256; used also for ʿnzˑti, "the god of Anzet," *T.* 146 = *M.* 199.

CLASS II. PARTS OF HUMAN FIGURE. PL. V.

head in profile, square beard and wig (black in *Ptahhetep*) in outline, beard often barred: **fig. 36**, *Pth.*, xxxix., right, 3; in one exceptional instance in *Akht.* hair detailed with locks. Word-sign for *tp*, "head," written ☺, and for its derivative ☺ *tpi*. As only very late variants are known, it is not quite certain whether in O.K. the first consonant of *tp* was *t*, *d*, or *z*; see *P. S. B. A.*, 1899, 269. Elsewhere det. of head, including *ḥ'*, "occiput," from which it is later transferred to *ḥ'*, "behind," &c.

(*Hier.*, p. 11); face showing beard and ears, but no hair: **fig. 41**, *Pth.*, xxxi., col. 3; **fig. 43**, *ib.*, xxxix., right, 4—beard barred.

(*Hier.*, p. 12); eye, black outline and ball, red in corner: **fig. 32**, *Akht.*; in two instances on false door of Ptahhetep (pl. xxxix.) pupil omitted. Common word-sign but not phon. In *m'*, "see," it may be taken as word-sign or as det. of , but = *m''*, the geminated form (SETHE, *Verbum*, i., § 390; *Siut*, i. 4).

eye with line drawn beneath in stibium: **fig. 33**, *Akht.* (offerings). Det. of *mˑsdmˑt*, "eye-paint," for which it is also used as word-sign in lists of offerings (*B. H.*, I., xvii., xxxv.). Elsewhere det. of *sdm*, "to paint the eye."

(*Hier.*, p. 12); lips of mouth: **fig. 52**, *Akht.*

mouth with curved stream of liquid (blue): **fig. 51**, *Pth.*, xli. 7; **fig. 54**, *ib.*, 19. No variants are known in lists of offerings. Elsewhere det. of "spittle"; *Pyr. W.* 15, *P.* 125 (also of *bš*, "vomit," *P.* 661, more rarely), so probably here also word-sign for same or for similar meaning, "washing, rinsing the mouth (?)." Cf. , **fig. 47**.

(*Hier.*, pp. 14-15); arms joined at shoulders, held up square, hands extended: **fig. 26**, *Pth.*, xxxix., right, 3; in xxxi. 3, 4, bracelets marked. Word-sign for *k'*, "worker (?)," the muscular life, energy and activity of man. Elsewhere phon. for *k'*. The arms seem to be represented in action, i.e. not in any attitude of rest, thus may correspond in some degree to Λ, the symbol of leg action. , **fig. 45**, *Pth.*, xxxiv. 1, same on sacred perch; also word-sign for the *ka*.

(*Hier.*, p. 14); compound of *k'* and the *ḥn* mallet = "*ka*-servant": **fig. 28**, *Pth.*, xxxiv. 3.

(*Hier.*, p. 14, with corn-rubber); arms with vase: **fig. 30**, *Pth.*, xli. 2. Word-sign for *sḥn*.

(*Hier.*, p. 15); arms holding shield and battle-axe (?): **fig. 46**, *Akht.* Note the late variant *yḥʿ*, where *y* stands for *'* as is shown by the demotic equivalent, and corresponds to O.K. ʿ (DARESSY, *Rec. de Trav.*, xvii., 113).

(*Hier.*, p. 15); two arms issuing from mouth (?) and grasping paddle: **fig. 53**, *Pth.*, xxxviii. 2.

(*Hier.*, p. 15); arm to shoulder holding *nḥbˑt*-wand, elbow obtusely bent, upper arm in full: **fig. 48**, *Pth.*, xli. 23, **fig. 49**, *ib.*, 20; in *Akht.* the crosspiece on the wand is very slight.

* ⎯◻ arm to shoulder, upper arm much abbreviated, elbow acutely bent, hand open and bent downwards: **fig. 35**, *Pth.*, xxxv. 3 (see "Corrections"); **fig. 37**, *ib.*, xxxviii. 3. Word-sign for *ḥs*, "sing," "make music," this action being accompanied by clapping of hands.

◻⎯◻ as last, but vase in hand, and elbow bent at right angles: **fig. 27**, *Pth.*, xxxii. 4; **fig. 31**, *ib.*, xxxix., l. 2. Word-sign for *ḥnk*, "offer ceremonially," with phon. trans.; used also for the derivative *m·ḥnk* (ERMAN and SETHE, *Ä. Z.*, xxxi. 97), perhaps meaning "artist-slave (?)" presented to a person (?), possibly "freedman." Combined with ☉☉☉, &c., det. of *w'g*, the name of a festival of offerings.

◻⎯◻ (*Hier.*, p. 15); as last, but hand receiving (?) gift: **fig. 34**, *Pth.*, xxxii. 2.

⎯◻ (*Hier.*, p. 12); arm cut off square above elbow, which is bent at right angles, the hand outstretched in line with fore-arm: **fig. 42**, *Pth.*, xxxix., right, 3. Phon. for ꜥ, Ar. ع.

⸝⎯◻ arm as last, water pouring over the open hand: **fig. 47**, *Pth.*, xxxvi. 2. In *Pyr.* the water often issues from a small vase. Used in writing ◊ ⸝⎯◻ *y'*, "wash," the water being det. Sometimes word-sign for same.

⊂⊃ (*Hier.*, p. 12); human hand open, cut off square at wrist: **fig. 29**, *Pth.*, xxxii. 3. Cf. SETHE, *Verbum*, i., 182-5, for a new view of its history.

* ◊ finger, showing nail: **fig. 39**, *Pth.*, xxxi. 4*a*; **fig. 40**, *Akht.* Word-sign for ⸘ ⎯ *zb'*, "finger," "digit-measure," "seal," "10.000." ◊, and more often ◊◊, the two fingers together, are det. of *'q'*, "exact," "corresponding"; probably the notion is in each case "exactness," and the two fingers may represent those which steady or make straight the plummet of the

balance, as represented in weighing scenes: or simply the notion of tallying.

⋀ legs to thighs, striding: **fig. 59**, *Pth.*, xxxii. 3. Rare det. of "be swift," "stride," "dart forward."

⌇ leg to above knee, bent: **fig. 44**, *Pth.*, xxxviii. 1. Word-sign for (1) *rd*, "foot" (cf. ⎯◻ and ⊂⊃, both for "hand," *Hier.*, p. 12); (2) *w'r·t*, "leg," from *w'r*, "run away," "flee"—with rad. ext. and phon. trans.; (3) *gḥs*, "gazelle"—as a swift runner—with phon. trans. (ERM., *Pap. Westc. Comm.*, p. 23) always distinguished by the phonetic complement *s*. Det. of leg, and in rather late times of verbs of running and walking.

⌇ (*Hier.*, p. 12); conventional "foot," the leg cut off square below the knee: **fig. 56**, *Pth.*, xxxii. 3.

⋀ (*Hier.*, p. 16); conventional "feet" joined below knee, as if in motion: **fig. 57**, *Pth.*, xxxii. 3. For the value ◊ ⧽ ⋀ *yw*, see also *Pyr. W.* 278, &c., and cf. SETHE, *Verbum*, i., 68, note 1, and 287.

⧈ **fig. 50**, *Pth.*, xli. 7; ⧆ **fig. 58**, *Pth.*, xxxiv. 2; ⧆ **fig. 55**, *Pth.*, xli 6; ◊ **fig. 38**, *Akht.*—for all these see *Hier.*, p. 16, under ⋀.

⌇ (*Hier.*, p. 16): **fig. 60**, *Pth.*, xxxi. 2.

CLASS III. MAMMALS. PL. VI.

⊕ recumbent lion, as frequently sculptured in the round: **fig. 72**, *Pth.*, xxxiii. 3. Word-sign and phon. for *rw*. At Dêr el-Gebrawi (VIth Dyn.) and later, the sculptured lion as the image of a god, &c., is named ⊕◊◊⧽, which is probably to be divided into *Rw-'bw* "lion-

c

leopard " (cf. *leo-pardus*)—see also Spiegelberg, *Rec. de Trav.*, xvii. 96; but apparently this name was not applied to living animals before the Roman period, when, in demotic, it indicates an animal (leopard?) associated with lions as a furious wild beast. Perhaps the close-maned lion was thought to be a different species from the great royal lion *mꜣ*. In *Tdtb.* there is a deity [glyph], presumably imagined in lion form and reading *Rw*.

Another word-sign or phonetic value is *ꜥr*, *ꜥrr*; Br., *Wtb.*, 205, quotes *ꜥr* as a name of the lion, but the reference given is not intelligible. The O.K. word [glyph] for a stela or false door (*Una*, ll. 7, 39) read *ꜥrrwt*, *ꜥrwt* (?); cf. [glyph], [glyph] in *Pyr.* = "door" (?): perhaps the entrance was guarded by lion-figures. In M.K. the word was commonly written [glyph] (M. Müller, *Ä.Z.*, 1888, 90). This value seems confined to the root *ꜥrrwt*, *ꜥrryt*, which in *Pyr.* and later is often *ꜥrwt*, *ꜥryt*; in N.K., however, we have *ꜥr*, "reed-pen," perhaps so spelt in Mar., *Ab.*, i. 31a, unless the lion be here simply *rw*. [glyph] was often confounded with [glyph] in [glyph] *ꜥr*, "granary," through similarity in the hieratic forms and in the sounds, also with [glyph], *šnꜥ*, "stop," "prevent" (*r. Medum*, Pls. xii., xv.), through the hieratic and some connexion of idea.

[glyph] Anubis animal, standing, coloured black: **fig. 63**, *Pth.*, xxxiii., col. 8. Name [glyph], "wise" (not *wnš*, "jackal"), *Pyr.* P. 451; with rad. ext. It is among the non-mythical animals in *B. H.*, II., Pl. iv. In spite of its black colour and excessively slender proportions, the evidence seems to identify it with the *canis niloticus*, or Egyptian fox, and with no other Egyptian animal now extant can it be identified.

[glyph] the same animal recumbent, as if on a rock or raised platform (after O.K. usually on the sign of a chapel [glyph]), its tail hanging down, coloured black (as *Medum*, Pl. xiii., L., *D.*, ii. 20, 58): **fig. 61**, *Pth.*, xxxix., left, 1. Word-sign for [glyph] *Ynpw*, the name of Anubis, god of burial. In somewhat "sportive" hieroglyphs (*B. H.*, I., xvii. top left, xxxii. top left, &c.) word-sign for *ḥry sštꜣ*, "he who is over the secrets."

[glyph] (*Hier.*, p. 16); desert hare: **fig. 62**, *Pth.*, xxxii. 3; **fig. 65**, *ib.*, xxxix., left, 3.

* [glyph] bull on sacred perch (*Hier.*, p. 58), before it fish-skin *km* (*Hier.*, p. 23): **fig. 79**, *Pth.*, xxxiv. 1, cf. xxxv. 2. Perhaps reads *kꜣ km*, "black bull." Word-sign for name of Athribite nome, the Xth of Lower Egypt.

The same, with sickle-shaped object before it: **fig. 77**, *Pth.*, xxxv. 2. Many poor examples in *Akht*, in which the object in front is less definite and without indentation at base. As the O.K. form of the sign for the VIth nome of Lower Egypt is known as [glyph] from *Methen*, the present one may possibly correspond to [glyph] of the Ptolemaic nome-list as the name of the XIth nome of Lower Egypt.

* [glyph] led ox, hornless, with leading cord round its lower jaw, the same (?) cord being also passed many times round its neck: **fig. 69**, *Pth.*, xxxi. 3. Det. (xxxi. 2) and apparently word-sign for *ywꜣ*, "fat cattle."

Calf with legs tied for slaughter, leading cord round neck, short tail: **fig. 73**, *Pth.*, xli. 24. Part of det. to *štpt*, "choice viands."

Cow on sacred perch (*Hier.*, p. 58), young animal in front: **fig. 66**, *Pth.* xxxiv. top. The young animal may be its calf, or may indicate *ywr*, "conception." Id. of Sebennyte nome, XIIth of Lower Egypt.

(*Hier.*, p. 17); young of an ungulate animal, newly dropped, the legs gathered under: **fig. 71**, *Pth.*, xli. 8; **fig. 75**, *ib.*, 3; in **fig. 74**, *ib.*, xli. 1—from the group *yw'*—by exception the legs are outstretched downwards, as if in an effort to rise.

* gazelle (*Gazella dorcas*): **fig. 68**, *Akht.* Det. of gazelles.

(*B. H.*, iii., p. 4; *Hier.*, p. 68); oryx on sacred perch, vase or bundle of hay in front; **fig. 64**, *Pth.*, xxxv. 2. Id. of oryx-nome, XVIth of Upper Egypt; it is masc., cf. *B. H.*, i., Pl. viii., ll. 17-18, *M'hz* (?) *r zr-f.*

kid (not calf) with short upturned tail (cf. *Medum*, xiii., xv.; *Methen*, L., *D.*, ii. 4): **fig. 70**, *Pth.*, xxxiii. 5. Name, *ib.*, lit. "skipper(?)," *Sall.*, I., iv. 1; *Anast.*, iv. 15, 5, frequent as proper name, "Kid," in M.K., e.g. SH., *Eg. Ins.*, ii. 94. In O.K. word-sign for *ib.*, and in N.K. even phon. for same.

(*Hier.*, p. 17); ram with horizontal horns, black on hind quarters and legs from shoulders: **fig. 76**, *Pth.*, xxxviii. 1. Word-sign for *B'*, the ram of Mendes (*Medum*, Pl. xxi.), so also probably in *Pth.*, xxxvii., xxxviii. The name *sr* occurs in *Pyr.*, as Max Müller pointed out.

ass (*Equus onager*): **fig. 67**, *Akht.* Word-sign for "ass."

CLASS IV. BIRDS. PLS. VII., VIII.

vulture (*Gyps*): **fig. 116**, *Akht.*; **fig. 117**, *Pth.*, xxxiii., col. 2 (in *ib.*, xxxii., col. 2, the leg-feathers and feet are blue, the body spotted). Name *nr't*. Word-sign for *nr*. Word-sign for *m't* or *mw't* (?), "mother." For the reading note that in *Prisse*, x. 3, "mother" is written

mt (or *mt't*?) instead of *mw't* (?), and the variant as early at least as Akhenaten is noteworthy. Occasionally in *Pyr.*, &c., phon. for plural ending of fem. words ending in *m't* (*Pyr.*, *knm'wt*, *Ssm'wt*, *P.* 319, *yhm'wt*, and L., *D.*, ii. 133a (Chnemhetep) even *mszm'wt*). Horapollo (i. 11) says that the vulture was considered to be only female. The goddess Nekheb·t, to whom the vulture was sacred, was called by the Greeks Eileithyia, though very little is known from Egyptian (cf. *P.S.B.A.*, 1899, 277, for some slight evidence) to indicate that her functions were those of the Greek goddess. The value *m't*, *mw't*, "mother," probably took its origin in mythology.

(*alif*, *Hier.*, p. 19); Egyptian vulture (*percnopterus*): **fig. 80**, *Pth.*, xxxi. 2; **fig. 83**, *ib.*, xxxiv., col. 1; **fig. 85**, *ib.*, xxxiii., col. 1; **fig. 93**, *ib.*, xxxiii., col. 6; **fig. 95**, *ib.*, xxxiii., col. 6; **fig. 89**, *Akht.* In *Pth.* there are traces of blue colour on the wing. The figure is very variable, two main varieties being discernible: one shows the scanty feathers at the back of the head like a fringe (figs. 83, 89), the other, esp. fig. 85, is more like a kite, particularly about the eye, and without naked flesh.

(*tyw*, *Hier.*, p. 19); eagle (*aquila*): **fig. 88**, *Akht.* (88 and 89 are contiguous signs).

(*Hier.*, p. 20); sparrow-hawk: **fig. 103**, *Pth.*, xli., col. 3 (cartouche); blue above, in *Pth.* and *Akht.*

(*Hier.*, p. 60); same, on symbol of the West, which is ⌒ with ostrich feather in it upon a staff with streamer, cf. the hawk-perch and vars. of: **fig. 90**, *Pth.*, xxxiv., col. 2; **fig. 94**, *ib.*, xxxi., col. 5. The ⌒ is blue in *Pth.* Cf. below ⌒, p. 30. For reading *wnm*, note that in *Tdth.*, cap. 17 (NAV., ii. 51), a N.K. pap. has (i.e. *wnm't*: *Hier.*, p. 37) = "right" (fem. adj.). It is

c 2

doubtful whether *wnm*, "right hand," is really a form of *ymn*; it would rather seem that it means the "eating" hand, from *wnm*, "eat." In modern Egypt the right hand is reserved for eating, the left being used for unclean purposes (*v.* LANE, *Modern Egyptians*, ch. v., on taking food—Ed. 1871, p. 185). The variation of with in *Pyr.* is doubtless due to the confusion of two values having similar meanings.

hawk on perch = *ntr*, "god" (*Hier.*, p 46, *s.v.*), combined with *ḥr* (*Hier.*, p. 63), and det. of "mountain" or "desert": fig. 87, *Pth.*, xxxix., right, col. 3—the invariable form in Ptahhetep, though the published outlines at times wrongly omit the ◻. This ◻ is coloured red (desert) in *Akht.* For O.K. form *v.* *Hier.*, p. 63. Reads *ḥr-ntr*, "necropolis." Note that this word seems to be masc., while *ḥrti ntr*, "[necropolis-] mason," is probably derived from a fem. form, *ḥr-t-ntr*, having a more general significance, "that which belongs to a god."

owl (*Hier.*, p. 20): figs. 81, 82, *Pth.*, xxxv. 5, 6; fig. 92, *Akht.*; fig. 409 (coloured), *ib.*

(*Hier.*, pp. 20, 67); swallow: fig. 108, *Pth.*, xxxviii., col. 4; fig. 102, *Akht.* The example from *Akht.* is unsculptured, and sketched in black ink only; it is in this case det. of its name *mnw't*, "swallow" or "pigeon(?)," in a place name; the black bars are curious, and render the value and species uncertain. At any rate, it is not more like a pigeon than like a swallow.

combination of the above with (*Hier.*, p. 35): fig. 109, *Pth.*, xxxiii., col. 4. Reads *Ḥ·t-wr't*, the "*great Het.*"

Pigeon (*Columba livia*): fig. 113, *Pth.*, xli. 14.

Det. of its name, *mnw't*, in the offerings: in *Akht.* called in the corresponding place *mn·t*, like the swallow.

(*Hier.*, p. 21); young unfledged bird, apparently taking and swallowing a worm; or young pigeon with its tongue out: fig. 86, *Akht.*, red skin with blue tail, wing feathers, &c.

(*Hier.*, p. 21); chick: fig. 98, *Pth.*, xxxii., col. 4—nearly uniform throughout the tomb: fig. 411, *Akht.* (coloured).

lapwing (*Vanellus cristatus*): fig. 84, *Akht.*; fig. 410, *ib.*, coloured, the colouring being fairly true to nature. Word-sign for *rḥy·t*, the name of the first of the three classes —not yet finally explained—into which the Egyptians divided mankind, or themselves alone. The Egyptian name of the bird is unknown—presumably it was *rḥy·t*.

(*Hier.*, p. 21); *ba*-plover: fig. 105, *Akht.*, ink only; fig. 114, *Pth.*, xli. 15—as usual in O.K. there is no tuft on the breast.

(*Hier.*, p. 21); sacred ibis (*Ibis religiosa*) on sacred perch: fig. 101, *Pth.*, xxxix., l. 2; fig. 112, *Akht.*, where the perch has the peculiar base elsewhere found with the ibis, e.g. *Medum*, xx., xxi.

(*Hier.*, p. 21); crested ibis (*Ibis comata*), traces of red colour all over in *Pth.* and *Akht.*: fig. 104, *Pth.*, xxxv. 5, in name "Akhethenem"; fig. 119, *ib.*, xxxv. 6; fig. 123, *ib.*, xxxviii. 1.

* head of crane (*Grus*): fig. 121, *Pth.*, xxxix., table of offerings. Used in offerings as word-sign for its name *z'·t*.

* (*Hier.*, p. 22); egret (?) swallowing fish: fig. 107, blue on wing, *Pth.*, xli. 7.

Goose with cut off head: **fig. 122**, *Pth.*, xli. 21. Together with ⊌ forms det. of *ḥnk·t*, "offering."

⟋ head of goose: **fig. 97**, *Pth.*, xxxix., offerings (det. of *r*); **fig. 99**, *ib.*, *l.c.* (det. or word-sign for *trp* in abbreviation), cf. *Hier.*, p. 23.

⟋ goose: **fig. 110**, *Pth.*, xli. 10 (det. of *r*); **fig. 118**, *ib.*, *l.c.* 11 (det. of *trp*).

⟋ (*Hier.*, p. 22); pin-tailed duck (*Dafila acuta*): **fig. 96**, *Pth.*, xxxiv. 4, and **fig. 100**, *ib.*, xxxii. over son, in both instances word-sign for *s*', "son"; **fig. 115**, *ib.*, xli. 12, det. of *s·t*, the name of the bird. Whether this is the bird that is word-sign for *'pd*, "bird" (*Pyr.*, *W.* 477, &c., &c.), is not quite clear.

⟋ (*Hier.*, p. 23); pin-tailed duck, flying: **fig. 106**, *Pth.*, xli. 21.

⟋ pin-tailed duck with wings over back, dropping on to water or hovering before settling: **fig. 91**, *Pth.*, xxxii. 3. Word-sign or det. of *ḥn*, "settle," "hover," with rad. ext.; · det. also of *nš*, "flutter." For use of this sign in combination with ⟋ *v. Hier.*, p. 52.

⟋ widgeon (?) (*Mareca penelope*): **fig. 111**, *Pth.*, xli. 13. Word-sign for its name *sr*; probably it is also word-sign for *wš'* (*Hier.*, p. 23).

⟋ trussed duck on stand: **fig. 120**, *Pth.*, xxxix., in offerings—perhaps picture rather than word-sign (the bird chrome yellow). In *ib.*, xli. 24, together with bound ox, it forms det. of *štp·t*, "choice viands."

CLASS V. PARTS OF MAMMALS. PL. IX.

⟋ (*Hier.*, p. 16); forepart of lion: **fig. 133**, *Pth.*, xli. 23.

⟋ hind quarters of leopard (?): **fig. 129**, *Pth.*, xxxv. 2. The tail is never as in ⟋ Name *ph*, "hinder part," also fem. *ph·t*. Word-sign for *ph*, with rad. ext. and phon. trans. Also word-sign for ⟋ *kf'*, perhaps on account of this word meaning, *inter alia*, "bottom of a jar," as opposed to ⟋ "top" (*Pap. Eb.*).

⟋ lion-skin: **fig. 138**, *Pth.*, xxxv. 3. Unusual det. of name of lion *m'*, occurring in proper name.

⟋ (*Hier.*, p. 19); hide of panther (?), tail curved or straight: **fig. 142**, *Pth.*, xxxix., l. 3; **fig. 143**, *ib.*, xxxii., col. 3.

⟋ (*Hier.*, p. 19); arrow piercing hide: **fig. 141**, *Pth.*, xxxii. 5.

⟋ (*Hier.*, p. 18); hide wrapped together: **fig. 124**, *Akht.* Cf. PIEHL, *P.S.B.A.*, xii., pp. 376, 433.

⊌ head of ox: **fig. 130**, *Akht.* Other instances *Pth.*, xxxiv. 4; *ib.*, xxxviii. 4. In offerings word-sign for *yw'*, "ox." In *Siut*, Tomb v. 16, it is det. of *qn*, "powerful," "victorious," the head being the formidable part of a fighting bull.

⟋ pair of ox-horns, with portion of skull adhering: **fig. 137**, *Pth.*, xxxv. 6. The crown of the head being named ⟋ *wp·t*, it is probably to this that the sign owes its word-sign value *wp*, "divide," "separate," &c., &c., though this value may be connected with the idea of "opening out," "parting" of horns. It appears to include also the value ⟋ *yp* where *y* remains firm, e.g. *yp·t* ⲟⲓⲟⲛⲉ (*yope*), "work," but not where it is modified to ⲛ: ⟋ with modified ⟋ is written ⟋. Cf. ⟋, ⟋.

Head and horns of oryx: **fig. 132**, *Pth.*, xxxviii. 4; also *ib.*, xxxiv. 4; in offerings word-sign for *m'ḥz*, "oryx."

◊ ear of ox, gazelle, or similar animal: **fig. 127**, *Pth.*, xxxiii. 1. Word-sign for ꟷ, "hear"; also for ꟷ "act as substitute," "lieutenant," probably from idea of "obedience," "hearkening to the order" of the person who appoints the substitute. Det. of ear, of ꟷ "deaf," of ꟷ "whisper (?)."

ꟷ tusk of hippopotamus (?) or elephant, conventionally figured: **fig. 126**, *Akht.* Word-sign for *ybḥ*, "tooth," whence phon. *bḥ*. Word-sign also for name of the god "*Ḥu*," apparently the god of the actions of the mouth—taste, speech, &c.; later with phon. trans. Det. of biting.

ꟷ tongue, conventionally represented with root and a prominence on the top at some distance from the root: **fig. 136**, *Pth.*, xxxii., col. 3. Name *nś·t*, "tongue." Word-sign and phon. for *nś*. Det. of "tongue" in *dp*, "taste," &c. After O.K. in hieroglyphic, word-sign for *mr*, "superintendent" (but never so used in hieratic); this may be a pun *m r*, "in the mouth," i.e. "tongue," or it may arise from a curious transference connected with *n-sw*, "to him belongs," which is written with ꟷ; for *n-sw* see SETHE, *Ä. Z.*, 1895, 73.

▽ female breast or teat: **fig. 125**, *Pth.*, xxxiii. 5. Det. of "breast." Name ꟷ "breast." Det. and occasional word-sign for *mnꜥ·t*, "a nurse," *Ä. Z.*, 1891, 102. In the present example its meaning as det. of *śś·t* is not quite certain: possibly it is here the vase-det. of the two kinds of *śś·t*-corn in the table of offerings.

ꟷ (*Hier.*, p. 18): **fig. 147**, *Pth.*, xli. 11.

ꟷ (*Hier.*, p. 17); shoulder and foreleg: **fig. 140**, *Pth.*, xli. 24.

ꟷ (*Hier.*, p. 18); shoulder (?) joint, trimmed and shrunk by boiling: **fig. 145**, *Pth.*, xli. 4.

Haunch (?) (always a more solid joint than that of previous sign) on sacred perch: **fig. 134**, *Akht.*; see also *Pth.*, xxxiv., top, and cf. *Methen*, L., *D.*, ii. 3. Id. for Letopolite, IIIrd nome of Lower Egypt; reading unknown.

ꟷ (*Hier.*, p. 18); rib: **fig. 144**, *Pth.*, xli. 4. Reads *śpr*, the *r* remaining firm in Coptic.

ꟷ (*Hier.*, p. 65); heart and windpipe rather than lute: **fig. 131**, *Pth.*, xli., col. 4.

ꟷ (*Hier.*, p. 18); heart: **fig. 135**, *Pth.*, xxxiv. 2, brownish colour.

ꟷ intestines (?) conventionally represented: **fig. 128**, *Pth.*, xxxiii. 5. (1) Name *qb*, *qꞌb*, "intestines," lit. the "folded," "winding" thing. Word-sign with rad. ext. (2) Word-sign for *phr*, "be twisted," "revolve," &c.: this is the commonest value. (3) Word-sign for *dbn*, "to circle," &c. (SPIEG., *Rec. de Trav.*, xv., 145, 4). (4) Word-sign for ꟷ "be turned over" (ERMAN, *Westc. Pap.*, vi. 10, *Commentary*), as subst., "winding water-channel (?)," or perhaps "dyke," "bank." In O.K. the word-sign for *wdb* is written ꟷ (*q.v.*, fig. 219), but in M.K. hieratic it is commonly ꟷ, with rad. ext.; in *Pyr.* apparently ꟷ (ꟷ is false). Cf. ꟷ (ERMAN, *Westc. Pap.*, x. 2, *Comment.*).

ꟷ piece of flesh: **fig. 136**, *Pth.*, xli. 6; **fig. 146**, *ib.*, xxxiv. 2. Det. of flesh, limbs, &c. Name ꟷ *ywf* (?), "meat," "flesh," which group is used also in O.K. for ꟷ *yw-f*, "he is" (ERMAN, *Ä. Z.*, 1881, 42).

CLASS VI. LOWER ORDERS OF ANIMALS. PL. IX.

ꟷ crocodile: **fig. 157**, *Pth.*, xxxii. 2; see also *ib.*, xxxviii. 3, in which example the ear is as in **fig. 157**, and the jaw serrated. The ear is probably a false rendering by the artist of a model in which the large nuchal plates at the back of the head were conspicuously shown : they are thus shown also in the large examples represented in O.K. scenes. Name 𓄲𓄿 *msḥ* (𓄲𓄿, *Dend.*, Pl. xxxvii.D., l. 592 ; cf. SETHE, *Verbum*, i. 151), for which it may stand as word-sign (*Pap. Eb.*). Being the figure of an animal sacred to Sebek it commonly stands for his name, 𓆋𓏤 *sbk*. Word-sign for 𓄿𓏤 *sȝq*, "be armoured," "be cautious." Det. of 𓄿 *ʿf*, "to be greedy," "voracious," also of 𓄿 *ʿd*, "to be hasty," "greedy"; sometimes in late texts word-sign for the last. Doubled, 𓆓, it stands for 𓇋𓏏𓏭 *yty*, *ytw*, "king" (NAVILLE, *Ä. Z.*, 1882, 190), especially in M.K.—no doubt for some mythological reason. The name of *Anzt*, the territory of the god *Anzti* (Osiris?), whose figure also serves as det. of *yty*, is often determined by water, and the god perhaps took the form of a crocodile (see above, p. 15).

Crocodile's hind leg and foot : **fig. 154,** *Pth.*, xxxvi. 3. Det. of *mnt*, "hind leg," "haunch."

𓆈 (*Hier.*, p. 24) ; lizard (green, speckled with black) : **fig. 156,** *Pth.*, xxxviii. 1.

𓆙 (*Hier.*, p. 24) : **fig. 148,** *Pth.*, xxxix., right, 3.

𓆗 cobra rising with swollen hood, on or in a *nbt* basket (cf. *Hier.*, p. 56) : **fig. 160,** *Pth.*, xxxiv. 1. Word-sign for the cobra goddess, 𓇅𓏏 *Wȝzyt*. The group 𓆗, representing Nekhebt, the vulture-goddess of the South, with Wazyt, the cobra-goddess of the North, is to be read *nbti*, "the two mistresses" (DARESSY, *Rec. de Trav.*, xvii. 113 ; PIEHL, *P.S.B.A.*, xx. 198-201), just as 𓌂𓌂, representing the gods of the North and South, is to be read *nbwi*, "the two masters" (PIEHL, *l.c.*). Det. sometimes of the names of sacred serpents, e.g. *Pyr.*, 369, N. 703.

𓆓 (*Hier.*, p. 4) : **fig. 149,** *Akht.*

𓇀 tadpole : **fig. 153,** *Pth.*, xxxi. 5, first to right. Name 𓆐𓏤 *ḥfnw*; fem. *ḥfnnt* (*Pyr. T.*, 309). In M.K., *ḥfnr*, L., D., ii. 144, *s* ; *ḥfnw*, *Pap. Ebers*. By phon. trans. expresses 100,000, written *ḥfnw* in *Sall. Pap.* iii. 8, 10, &c.

𓆏 frog on *nbt* basket : **fig. 158,** *Pth.*, xxxii., col. 4. Symbol of frog-goddess *Ḥeqt*, and word-sign for her name.

𓆛 mullet (?) (*Arab. bûn*) *Mugil* : **fig. 151,** *Pth.*, xxxiii., col. 8. Coloured blue in *Pth.* and *Akht.* In the present instance word-sign in the title *sb ʿd mr*. Read 𓂝 (𓆛) *ʿd* ; cf. BERGMANN, *Rec. de Trav.*, vii. 179, and ostracon of Sanehat, l. 1 (*P.S.B.A.*, xiv. 455). The *ʿd*, or "piercer (?)" fish, is frequently referred to in XVIIIth Dyn. hymns in *Tdtb.*, and in N.K. fish accounts : it was commonly split and dried for food.

𓆟 (*Hier.*, p. 25) ; bulti-fish : **fig. 152,** *Akht.*

𓆤 bee : **fig. 161,** *Pth.*, xxxi. 2. Its name is probably given by 𓆤𓏤 "bee," as symbol of the King of Lower Egypt (*Kah. Pap.* iii., l. 2). The reading until recently has been very doubtful. The sign stands for "king," and for "honey," &c. In Coptic "honey" is ⲉⲃⲓⲱ (*ebyô*); hence SETHE, *Ä. Z.*, 1890, 125, concluded that 𓇋𓏏𓇯 *byty*, used as the title of the King of Lower Egypt in *Pyr. T.*, 352, was an alphabetic transcript of 𓆤𓏤. (The latter has since been found as its equivalent in a very debased copy of the same text, MÖLLER, *Ä. Z.*, 1897, 166.) MAX MÜLLER, *Ä. Z.*, 1892, 56, confirmed Sethe's view, chiefly by quoting alliterative plays on the same royal title with the word for "honey" and with *yb*, "heart." The place-name, 𓆤𓈖𓏤, with numerous variants, is to be read *ȝḫ-byt*, "Papyrus Clump of the Bee," or "of the Bee-King(?)"; in late times it was reduced to *ḥb·t*, and so commonly spelt out (SETHE, *Ä. Z.*, 1892, 114). See also PIEHL, *Ä. Z.*, 1898, 85. The only point still doubtful is whether (*y*)*byt*—as Max Müller preferred—or *byt* is to be read. *byty* is King of Lower Egypt; pl. *byt·yw*. In *Pap. Harr.* i. there is a class of people, perhaps those who collected gum from the trees, named *byty*(?). The *basse-époque* use of the bee as word-sign for *k'·t*, "work" (BR., *Wth. Suppl.*, 1231) is interesting.

dung-beetle (*Scarabaeus sacer*); black in Pth.: **fig. 155**, *Pth.*, xxxvi. 3. The animal, though inconspicuous in itself, is very noticeable for its habits. Name *ḫprr* (*Pyr. W.*, 447 = N., 747). Word-sign for *ḫpr*, by the usual loss of the doubled consonant.

(*Hier.*, p. 25); bivalve shell: **fig. 150**, *Pth.*, xli. 15; **fig. 159**, *Akht.* Compare the shell hung round the neck of the ox, amongst the miscellaneous details, Pl. xvi.A top right.

CLASS VII. VEGETATION. PL. X.

four-petalled flower, open: **fig. 187**, *Akht.* Word-sign for *wn*, "to open." Phon. for *wn*, most frequently so used in O.K.; later almost confined to *wm*, "eat," where it gradually changed its form to (*q.v. Hier.*, p. 37).

fig. 167, *Pth.*, xli. 2. Det. of *d'b*, "fig," whether *Ficus carica* or *Ficus sycomorus*.

(*Hier.*, p. 26); pod of carob bean: **fig. 181**, *Akht.* (green). Word-sign for "sweet," "pleasant"; whether this value is due to the "sweetness" of the pod, or to the tree itself being called *ss-wzm*, in late times *wtm*, is not clear.

grains of corn; **fig. 171**, *Pth.*, xli. 14. Word-sign for *yt*, "barley" (*Pyr. M.*, 20 = N., 119, &c. In early times det. of corn, afterwards superseded by .

Stand with grain: **fig. 177**, *Pth.*, xli., offerings 24. Det. of *pḥ'*, probably a grain used in beer-making.

(*Hier.*, p. 27); threshing-floor: **fig. 190**, *Pth.*, xxxiii. 5.

(the flower(?) , *Hier.*, p. 26, is a form of it) root(?): **fig. 184**, *Pth.*, xli. 19. Word-sign for *bn(r)*, "sweet," "date," &c.: possibly a sweet root such as beet-root (*Beta*).

Bunch of onions on a basket: **fig. 175**, *Pth.*, xli. 19. Det. of *ḥz·w*, "onions."

(*Hier.*, p. 26); trimmed branch or tree-stem: **fig. 179**, *Pth.*, xxxix., col. 8; **fig. 168**, *Akht.* (only one instance of this form in the tomb).

tree: **fig. 188**, *Pth.*, xli. 16; **fig. 191**, *ib.*, 10. (In the first instance the name is *nbs*, in the second *ysd*.) Det. of trees. Word-sign for "pleasant," "graceful," and a kind of tree so called, with rad. ext. and phon. trans. In *Pyr.*, det. of *qb*, "refreshing."

tree on sacred perch: **fig. 178**, *Akht.* Nome-sign, perhaps the same as the next.

The same, with ill-defined appendage, which in the best instances in *Akht.* resemble a human arm and hand holding : **fig. 174**, *Pth.*, xxxv. 2, no. 3; **figs. 186, 192**, *Akht.* There are cases in which the appendage looks like a flower on a curved stem. Nome-sign, probably for XXth and XXIst nomes of Upper Egypt.

༒ (cf. *B. II.*, iii., fig. 28); vine on props :
fig. 166, *Pth.*, xxxiii. 6—props red, vine green,
with dull maroon longitudinal stripes, bunches
of fruit blue ; **fig. 173**, *ib.*, xxxiii. 5, coloured
in **fig. 405**. In offerings word-sign for 🍷 ,
" wine." Det. of *yrr·t*, " vine," *k'n*, " garden,"
and of names of many garden fruit-trees,
especially in hieratic.

༒ (*Hier.*, p. 26); herb : **fig. 163**, *Pth.*,
xxxv. 6. Det. of a plant-name, *stf*, used as a
proper name. In *Akht.* det. of *ynb*-plant in
proper name. In *Pth.*, xxxii. 3, the injured
hn-plant sign (see " Corrections," p. 42) is of the
same type as in *Medum*, pl. xv.

༒ lotus-leaf : **fig. 165**, *Pth.*, xxxviii., below
table; green with brown stem. Word-sign for
h', " leaf," of lotus and melon (*Pap. Eb.* and
Sign Pap.). Phon. for *h'*.

༒ (*Hier.*, p. 28); clump of three papyrus
stems : **fig. 165**, *Pth.*, xxxi. 2. Det. and later
word-sign for *T'-mh*, the " North-Land," where
papyrus was chiefly grown, and for *mh*,
" North." Word-sign for *h'*, " behind," in *Pth.*,
xli. 20.

༒ clump of papyrus with buds bent down :
fig. 162, *Akht.*; **fig. 169**, *Pth.*, xxxiv. 1.
Word-sign for *y'h*, " be verdant " (*Pth.*, *l.c.*);
later written *w'h*, and then *w'rh*. Det. " papy-
rus-marsh(?)," *zt*. In *Akht.* frequent in group
= " North," or " papyrus-marsh."

༒ (*Hier.*, p. 28); stem of papyrus : **fig. 172**,
Pth., xli. 12.

༒ (*Hier.*, p. 28); conventionalized rush (?)
(on N. wall Ptahhetep, coloured green with blue
tips); **fig. 170**, *Pth.*, xxxii. 3.

༒ (*Hier.*, p. 29); royal plant of South-Land :
fig. 185, *Pth.*, xxxiii., col. 8.

༒ (*Hier.*, p. 29); sedge in flower (?); **fig.176**,
Pth., xxxv., col. 1; **fig. 182**, *ib.*, xxxi. 2—green,
flowers and roots red (?), base blue.

༒ same plant as last, but with ∩ = 10 sub-
stituted for base: **fig. 180**, *Pth.*, xxxix., right 2.
Compound word-sign for *mz·t*(?) *qm'*, " tens of
the South," in a title the plural of which is
written (*Wuzir* inscr. in Tomb
Amenemapt, ed. NEWBERRY, l. 2).

༒ three reed-flower heads, with lines of
somewhat uncertain meaning connecting and
between them : **fig. 189**, *Akht.* Word-sign for
sh·t, " meadow-land," and *sm*, " herbage."

༒ (*Hier.*, p. 27); reed-head in flower, the
feathery head treated like the true feather ༒;
fig. 164, *Akht.*

CLASS VIII. EARTH, WATER, AND SKY.
PL. XI.

☉ (*Hier.*, p. 30); disk of the Sun : **fig. 214**,
Pth., xxxiii., col. 7.

༒ disk on ༒ (*q.v. Hier.*, p. 63): **fig. 221**,
Akht., coloured, fig. 403. Compound word-sign
for *hr·t hrw*, " that which belongeth to the
day."

༒ crescent moon : **fig. 200**, *Pth.*, xxxiii.,
col. 3; **fig. 201**, *ib.*, xli. 18; in the first
instance, value *y'h*, in the second *w'h*. Occasionally det. and word-sign for *y'h*, " moon "
(*Pyr. P.*, 279), but in that case usually taking
a less conventionalized form or position, e.g.
), ⌒. Probably ⌒, the word-sign for *w'h*,
hw', the name of a kind of grain, is the same
sign. In *Merab*, L., D., ii. 19, as the month-
sign it is coloured white; the *w'h* is half
black, half yellow, in L., D., ii. 70, and, as
Mr. Newberry informs me, yellow in the tomb

of Rekhmara (XVIIIth Dyn.). In spite of these differences it seems evident that one sign spells both wch and y^ch (cf. below ⌒). SETHE, *Verbum*, i., §§ 202, 253, 10, believes that wch was a more ancient form of y^ch, and connected with Semitic names of the moon. In abbreviated writing of dates, ⌒ is word-sign for *ybd* (?), "month," the last radical being shown in the common variant ⌣, while the other radicals are indicated by a very late variant ⌢ ⌣, for *ybt*, "net" (BR., *D. G.*, 1078), and by Copt. ⲉⲃⲟⲧ, "month," though the semi-consonant is of course rather uncertain.

⌢ crescent with star: **fig. 198**, *Pth.*, xxxix. l. 2. Specific word-sign for *ybd*, "month."

⌢ half crescent with star: **fig. 193**, *Pth.*, xxxix., l. 2. Word-sign for half-month, i.e. 15th day.

∿ (*Hier.*, p. 30); hilly desert, spotted red, with green base: **fig. 212**, *Pth.*, xxxix., left, 1.

∿ same on staff or perch: **fig. 208**, *Pth.*, xxxiii., col. 4, symbol with ostrich feather at end on staff with streamer beneath: **fig. 216**, *ib.*, xxxix., l. 3, on hawk-perch, the crossbar above not indicated. Word-sign—so far as is known—not for a district but for the name of a god, viz. that of the VIth nome ⌔ of Lower Egypt. His name reads ⌔, *Pyr. N.*, l. 850 = ⌔ *M.*, l. 331, *r.* MASP., *Ét. Eg.*, ii. 265; BR., *P. S. B. A.*, x. 450; PIEH·, *Sphinx*, i. 62.

∿ (*Hier.*, p. 31); two-crested mount, spotted red, with green base: **fig. 210**, *Pth.*, xxxix., left, 1.

◿ (*Hier.*, p. 32); mound of earth: **fig. 217**, *Pth.*, xxxix., right 4; **fig. 220**, *ib.*, xxxi., col. 4 (blue). A good instance of its biliteral value

◿ is in ◿◿ (*Pth.*, xxxi.) = $q^{\prime}q^{\prime}$ (*Berl. Pap.*, ii. 35).

◿(?) probably a totally different sign from the last. In *Medum*, Pl. xi., it is large and white. An instrument for taking angles (?): **fig. 196**, *Akht*. Word-sign for *wḥr·t*, "workshop (?)"; cf. *Pth.*, xxxv.; *Mera*, p. 549; in *Pap. Harr.* seems to mean "wood-yards."

◿◿ (*Hier.*, p. 32); double ⸝—two heaps of provisions (?): **fig. 209**, *Pth.*, xli.; offerings, 22.

Triple heap: **fig. 207**, *Pth.*, xli.; offerings, 22. Peculiar det. of heaps of provisions (?). Cf. L., *D.*, ii. 70, ◿◿◿ (black); *r.* ♃, *Hier.*, p. 32.

⌢ (*Hier.*, p. 32); flat land, blue; **fig. 204**, *Pth.*, xxxi. 2; *r.* ⌒.

⊟ (*Hier.*, p. 33); divided land (?): **fig. 206**, *Akht*, **fig. 215**, *Akht*. Nome det.; in *Pth.* the nome is imperfect, presumably the halberd. It seems possible that some varieties of this sign are to be connected with a draught-board.

⌒ piece of bank, or water, straight at one end and tapering to the other, which is rounded: **fig. 219**, *Pth.*, xxxi. 3; red with green spots. The same sign shown in *B. H.*, ii., pl. vii. (towards the left) is white dotted with red (CHAMP., *Not.*, ii. 373), but according to an old note of my own it is filled with vertical ripple-lines in the IVth Dyn. stela of Mer-hest in the Gizeh Museum. Word-sign for its name ⌔, first read by MASPERO, cf. *Pyr. M.*, 194, and L., *D.*, ii. 84; *Pyr. M.*, 343, and the common title ⌔, also MASP., *Ét. Eg.*, ii. 207; later usually written ⌔. The meaning is probably "shore," "bank" of river or sea. Probably the same as ⌔ = ⌔ (cf. y^ch = w^ch); possibly, also, the M.K. geographical det. ⌒ is derived from it.

tank (?): **fig. 213**, *Akht.* In O.K. frequent in estate names. In *Methen*, L., D., ii. 7*b*, ▭, sometimes without detail ▭, is clearly distinguished from ▦, and from ▦ = *sp'·t* (?), L., D., ii. 7*c*. The sign may represent a dry tank or pool excavated with sloping sides, while ▦ is the same full of water. Cf. the sign ▭ *grg* in *Methen*, L., D., ii. 6, 7, which may represent a ditch in course of excavation by means of a mattock. In *Methen*, L., D., ii. 3, it seems several times to be word-sign for the measure of area called *st·t*, ἄρουρα, of 100 cubits square (cf. *P. S. B. A.*, xiv. 412). In the estate names from *Methen*, ▭, ▭, ▤, ▤, all occur, but the associated consonants are not merely phonetic complements.

▭ (*Hier.*, p. 33); tank with water—all blue: **fig. 205**, *Pth.*, xxxiii. 2; in *Pth.*, xxxviii. 4, crossed with ripple lines.

▤ rectangular space filled with water: **fig. 218**, *Pth.*, xxxii., col. 2—water blue, the bounding lines (blue for land) above and below projecting at either end, and indicating indefinite extension (cf. ▦). Name *mr*, "channel," "canal." Word-sign for *mr*, "love," &c.; rarely used phonetically for ▦ [▭] = ▦ = ▦ in ▤, ▤, ▤, &c. In *Pth.*, xxxiv. 2, there is an instance in which the sculptor has wrongly cut it down to ▭.

▭ curved canal, resembling the last: **fig. 202**, *Pth.*, xxxix., right, 3; the interior (water) blue. The curve is as in some early forms of ▦, e.g. in stela of Merhest, Gizeh Mus. Unusual det. of *by'*; meaning uncertain.

▽ (*Hier.*, p. 33); pool: **fig. 195**, *Pth.*, xxxix., right, 3—blue inside. Same form in all cases: as regards the instance in *Pth.*, xli., offerings, 18, like an axe-head with loops, the original shows it to be incorrectly drawn; it is, in fact, as in fig. 195. Word-sign for *hm* and *by'*.

〰 (*Hier.*, p. 33); ripple-line: **fig. 211**, *Pth.*, xxxix., left, 3; black in *Pth.*

▭ mud floor, brick (?): **fig. 197**, *Pth.*, xxxv. 4, det. of *h'y·t.*

°°° three balls: **fig. 194**, *Pth.*, xli. 5.

° pellet, coloured yellow: **fig. 203**, *Pth.*, xxxix., table of offerings. Det. of *s·ntr*, "incense" (cf. *Hier.*, p. 34).

CLASS IX. BUILDINGS AND THEIR PARTS.
PL. XII.

⊗ (*Hier.*, p. 34); plan of village: **figs. 231** and **404** (coloured), *Akht.*; in one example in *Akht.* red takes the place of black.

△ pyramid conventionally represented, acutely pointed, with a level base or platform; **fig. 226**, *Akht.*, dividing lines above base and below apex; **fig. 246**, *Pth.*, xxxiii., col. 6, apex divided off by a line. The lines no doubt indicate casings of different colours, as in the example from *Akht.*, **fig. 400** (coloured). The basal band is coloured to imitate granite, while in the example from Ptahhetep the apex appears to show traces of yellow. Det. of "pyramid," the Egyptian name of which was *mr.*

▦ (*Hier.*, p. 34); wall: **fig. 240**, *Akht.* From nome-sign of Memphite nome.

▦ (*Hier.*, p. 34); plan of palatial courtyard: **fig. 222**, *Pth.*, xxxiii., col. 2, group ▦; **fig. 223**, *ib.*, xli. 17; **fig. 225**, *Akht.*, with complete square. In the coloured example, **fig. 406**, *Akht.*, the detail is remarkable, with *hz* between two eyes. In the same tomb there is another similar example, and another without the ▯ but with the eyes.

⊓ (*Hier.*, p. 35); plan of plain double court-yard: **fig. 243**, *Pth.*, xxxix., left, 3. One example in Ptahhetep is coloured blue for brick.

⊔⊓ plan of zig-zag wall (?): **figs. 227**, *Pth.*, xxxix. (in canopy), and **244** (coloured blue), *Pth.*, xxxix., left 4. Word-sign for *nm*, "wander round," &c.; with rad. ext. After O.K. word-sign for *mr·t*, meaning perhaps a winding passage or street; with rad. ext. and phon. trans. as *mr*.

⊓ (*Hier.*, p. 35); plan of enclosure with building in the corner: **fig. 228**, *Pth.*, xxxi. 2. Three conjoined for plural.

The same, enclosing royal name *S'ḥw-Rˁ*; **fig. 252**, *Pth.*, xxxiv., top.

⊏⊐ (*Hier.*, p. 35); plan of chamber (?): **fig. 234**, *Pth.*, xxxix., right, 3 (blue); **fig. 238**, *Akht.*

⊏⊥⊐ the same, with oar, *ḫrw*: **fig. 236**, *Pth.*, xxxix., left, 3. Abbreviation for *pr ḫrw*, "utterance of the voice," "utterance of summons"; later extended as *pr·t r ḫrw*, "coming out to the voice." See *P. S. B. A.*, 1896, 198 (much of the explanation uncertain).

plan of chamber or court, one wall of which is shown as crested with serpents: **figs. 230, 232**, *Akht.*; wall blue, serpents yellow. Cf. *Medum*, pl. xxi., and in Mr. Newberry's *Rekhmara*, pl. iv. Word-sign for *t'* (?), *t'·t* (?), "royal court of justice (?)," Mar., *Ab.*, i. 19a. In late times varying with — *t'*, *t*, Br., *Wtb. Suppl.* 389, 1306, 1036. In *Tdtl.* the façade of shrines of divinities, especially that of Osiris as king, is often crowned with uraei: so also is the Hall of the Two Truths.

(*Hier.*, p. 36); gate or hut-shrine (?): **fig. 245**, *Pth.*, xxxix., left, 1. In demotic *syḫ-ntr*

corresponds to in the title of Anubis (*Dend.*, pl. xxv., &c.), suggesting — as the reading, but demotic equivalents in such cases are not to be altogether trusted.

Pole on forked uprights—probably those of the wine-press—between which is seen a hut-shrine (?): **fig. 251**, *Pth.*, xxxiii. 5. Word-sign for name of a god of the vintage (?) , *Pyr. T.*, 324 = *W.*, 511 (Masp., *Ä. Z.*, 1882, p. 129), confirmed by the demotic spelling *śśm* (Br., *Zwei biling. Pap. (Rhind)*, vi. 2, x. 8. There is probably some mistake about the form *ḥnm·w*, noted *Kah. Pap.*, p. 104, as W. Max Müller has remarked to me.

(*Hier.*, p. 35): **fig. 247**, *Pth.*, xxxviii. 1; **fig. 249**, *ib.*, xxxix., l. 2.

Domed granary, trebled for the plural: **fig. 239**, *Pth.*, xxxiv., top. Det. of *mḫr*.

Circular tower (?), the upper part with traces of coloured bands: **fig. 242**, *Pth.*, xxxix., right, 4. In *ib.* left, 4 (the published form is erroneous), slight traces of colour seem to show six horizontal bands, green and blue alternately.

⊂⊃ (*Hier.*, p. 37); block of stone: **fig. 224**, *Pth.*, xxxv. 6.

(*Hier.*, p. 37); upright cross: **fig. 235**, *Pth.*, xxxiii. 5.

✕ diagonal cross: **fig. 237**, *Pth.*, xxxii. 5. (1) Indicates quartering. In hieratic it is the sign for ¼, but has not yet been found in hieroglyphic where *r-ifd* takes its place. In Pellegrini, *Insc. di Palermo*, pl. ii., apparently some measure of area. Perhaps from this arithmetical use it became word-sign for *ḥsb*, "count," though it was gradually replaced by

◯ (*q.v. Hier.*, p. 63). Det. of *ḫb*, "subtract," of *pss*, "divide"; also for multiplication and abundance (◬ ⌇). This sign also conveys, as crossed sticks, the idea of (2) crossing—det. of *z'*, "traverse"—and (3) of going different ways, departure, opening doors, ⊠ , ⋀ = *sw'*, "pass away" (M.K., *Sanehat*, l. 290), and × ⌇ *sw'*, "cut down," "cut off," in N.K. Here also, perhaps, belongs the meaning "division" (cf. N.K. × ∩ ⌒ = M.K. ⋁ ▢ ∩ ⌒ "separate them," "detail them"—of a list in detail) and "multiplication"; det. of *ḫb*, "subtract," *ss*, "open door." (4) Also of "mixing"; word-sign in N.K. for ×, ⌇ *sbn*, "mixed," and det. of *sb*, "mix." (5) × ⋒ , M. and N.K., reads *sz't* rather than *ḫ't*; cf. *Pyr. W.*, 184, with parallel at *Deir el Bahri*, also *Mentuhotep*, p. 24, no. 56, and *Peduamenap*, i., pl. xviii., no. 2. The origin of this last value of × is not yet explained.

| (*Hier.*, p. 37); unit line (piece of wood or clamp, but black in *Pth.*): **fig. 239***b*, *Pth.* xxxiii. 5; black.

▯ fluted wooden column tapering upwards, a tenon projecting at the top (*v. Medum*, Front., fig. 15, and p. 30, § 48): **fig. 229**, *Akht.*, **fig. 233**, *Pth.*, xxxii. col. 3. The fluting is most clearly shown in the example from Ptahhetep; that from Akhethetep (cf. *Pth.*, xli., col. 1) is conventionalized and with plain base. Name *yn* (no early variant, so the first element uncertain), "column," "support," with rad. ext. and phon. trans.

▯ (*Hier.*, p. 38); *seh*-pole placed upright, usually horizontal: **fig. 250**, *Pth.*, xxxviii., col. 2; red.

⟞ (*Hier.*, p. 38); door-bolt: **figs. 241, 248**, *Akht.* See a fine original figured by H. Towry White in *P. S. B. A.*, 1899, 286.

CLASS X. POTTERY, VASES, FIRE. PL. XIII.

◖ (*Hier.*, p. 39); jug with loop in front; **fig. 267**, *Pth.*, xxxiii. 6; an instance in xli. 6 is blue with stripe across.

◗ (*Hier.*, p. 39); *hes*-vase: **fig. 260**, *Akht.*

◗ (*Hier.*, p. 39); the same, with water pouring from it: **fig. 269**, *Akht.*

◗◗◗◗ (*Hier.*, p. 39); four *hes*-vases, with cloth or, as PIEHL suggests, indication of the case containing them; **fig. 265**, *Pth.*, xxxii. 5.

◖ beer-jug: **fig. 264**, *Pth.*, xxxvi. 5. In Ptahhetep, blue top; in Akhethetep, blue top, red below. Word-sign for *ḥqt*, "beer," in formulae of offerings (*Pth.*, xxxiv., xxxviii., under table), det. of beer. Word-sign for O. and M.K. title *dpw*, "taster"; cf. ⌁ ◖ *Pyr. W.*, 175 = ◖ ⌁ *Pyr. M.*, 636, and the other parallels. Cf. *Rhind Math.*, xx., no. 71, for the connexion of *dp*, "taste," with beer-making; see also BR., *Aeg.*, p. 225, who reads the sign *ybw*.

◑ (*Hier.*, p. 39); globular water-pot: **fig. 257**, *Pth.*, xxxii. 2; blue.

Nmst-vase (cf. *Hier.*, p. 42): **fig. 262**, *Pth.*, xli. 19. Det. of its name (*ib.*, 24), and of the *zsrt* drink.

Bowl: **fig. 254**, *Pth.*, xli. 6. Det. of *snw*, "doctor," "medicine." Perhaps the vase *snw* of L., *Ä. T.*, 43.

⊕⊕ double vase, one probably with clay cap, the other with ribbed neck: **fig. 253**, *Pth.*, xxxix., table; cf. *ib.*, xli. 4. Det. of *yrp*, "wine."

◗ (*Hier.*, p. 40); milk vase (?): **fig. 261**, *Pth.*, xli. 6; see below, p. 38.

▽ (*Hier.*, p. 42); *wsḫ*-bowl: **fig. 266**, *Pth.*, xxxiv. 4.

▽ (*Hier.*, p. 43, *s.v.*); censer, with ram: **fig. 256**, *Akht.* Word-sign for *b'*, "soul," with , and name of the sacred ram of Mendes; rare in O.K.

⊖ *wesekh* (?)-bowl, with another covering it, or loaf of bread moulded in two bowls: **fig. 268**, *Pth.*, xli., offerings, 19. Det. of *qmḥw qm'*.

▽ hand censer without its lid: **fig. 263**, *Akht.* Det. of *s·ntr-sz·t* in offerings.

⊠ (*Hier.*, p. 41); ring-stand, red in Ptah-hetep: **fig. 255**, *Pth.*, xxxii., col. 2 (*ws·t*); **fig. 258**, *ib.*, xxxiii. 5 (*g*).

□ (*Hier.*, p. 42); kiln: **fig. 259**, *Pth.*, xxxiii., col. 2; coloured in **fig. 399**.

(*Hier.*, p. 42); flaming brazier: **fig. 270**, *Pth.*, xli. 22. Note that *pfs* is a false form. In O.K. it was *fs* (Mera, 534, 564; SETHE, *Verbum*, i., § 216, 2); later *ps*, and sometimes it was confusedly written *pfs*. In N.K. stands for (root, *nsr·t*, "flame"), Horhotep, ll. 356-7 = *Tdtb.*, ch. xxiv.

CLASS XI. IMPLEMENTS AND TOOLS.
PL. XIII.

(*Hier.*, p. 48); sickle: **fig. 282**, *Pth.*, xxxix., right, 2; handle green, teeth white (?).

(*Hier.*, p. 48): wooden tied hoe: **fig. 283**, *Akht.*; **fig. 285**, *Pth.*, xxxix., left, 2.

(*Hier.*, p. 49); plasterer's float (?): **fig. 271**, *Akht.* Cf. a float figured in *Kahun*, ix. 10.

(*Hier.*, p. 49); *mr*-chisel: **fig. 278**, *Pth.*, xxxi., top; unsymmetrical, as usual in O.K., green handle, blue blade.

⌒ (*Hier.*, p. 49); drill-cap: **fig. 284**, *Pth.*, xxxix., right, 3—blue. In the ⌒ seems like a piece of clay: perhaps ⸺ is homophonous with it.

⌐ handle of adze: **fig. 276**, *Pth.*, xxxii. 2. In O.K. word-sign and phon. for *nw*; word-sign also for *'np't*, as name of the city of Mendes; probably for some mythological reason (*Medum*, Pl. xxi.). Later the sign became ⌒, ⌒; *c. Hier.*, p. 50.

Adze with triple (i.e. multiple) blade: **fig. 279**, *Pth.*, xxxiii. 6. In O.K. usual word-sign for *'n·t*, "claw," "nails"; *v. Hier.*, p. 50, *s.v.* ⌒; also LANGE, *Ä. Z.*, 1896, p. 77.

⌒ (*Hier.*, p. 50); adze cutting wood: **fig. 277**, *Pth.*, xli. 24.

adze and saw—rather than knife: **fig. 273**, *Pth.*, xxxv. 6, where it is followed by ⌑, a stone, and designates a mason. Occurs similarly in Thy. Reading unknown—might be *nzr* (?).

carpenter's axe: **fig. 280**, *Akht.*—blade apparently red. Cf. *Medum*, Front. 14, and Pl. x. Name, *myb·t*: tomb of Thy (BR., *Wtb.*, 583). Word-sign for "ship-building" and "carpentering"—especially of doors; probably reads *s'qh*, or *'qh*. BR., *Wtb.*, and BIRCH, *Dict.*, both quote *'qh* as the name of the war-axe, but the reference in each case is wrong, and cannot be verified. In MAR., *Ab.*, i. 8, l. 85, seems to occur, but the first sign is imperfect, while is used correspondingly at Dêr el Bahri (cf. NAVILLE and SETHE in *Arch. Rep.*, 1895-6, p. 8, note [2]). The corresponding hieratic word could be interpreted either as with ☞ or with ○ɣ. The supposed full spelling, ⎰ 🦅 ◿ 𒐰 ⌐, is given in the Antef stela (*T. S. B. A.*, 1875, 192), but this may be divided as *š-'ḥ*.

Polisher: **fig. 247**, *Pth.*, xxxviii. 2—brown (or red?). Word-sign for the title *sšp*, "polisher." ⌐ ▢, *Pyr. M.*, 607 = *P.*, 424.

◥ (*Hier.*, p. 50); knife: **fig. 286**, *Akht.*

◣▢ knife sharpener, pierced, and fitted with loop: **fig. 275**, *Pth.*, xxxviii. 2—blade brown(?); in the scenes in Akhethetep the blade of the sharpener is blue. In *Methen*, L., *D.*, ii. 3, a curved bar, with loop lashed to it. Cf. *B. H.*, iii., Pl. ix., figs. 3, 6, 7, and for its use, *ib.*, Pl. x. 2. As being constantly worn by butchers, it is word-sign for *sšm*, "butcher" (*Methen*, L., *D.*, ii. 4, and Thy; with phon. trans. For the proof of the reading *r.* MAX MÜLLER, *Rec. de Trav.*, xiv. 18. In N.K. it frequently has conventional feet attached, owing to its common meaning of "lead."

⎰ (cf. *Hier.*, p. 57, and below fig. 358); shepherd's crook: **fig. 281**, *Akht.* Word-sign for *'w·t*, "animals," "small cattle."

⎱ (*Hier.*, p. 50); fire-stick apparatus: **fig. 287**, *Pth.*, xxxix., right, 3. For expressions "striking" and "rubbing light" in Eg., cf. O. v. LEMM, *Ä. Z.*, 1887, 114; BR., *Thes.*, 470.

⎰ (*Hier.*, p. 51); support of balance: **fig. 272**, *Akht.*

CLASS XII. CORDAGE, TEXTILE-WORK, &c.
PL. XIV.

⎰ (*Hier.*, p. 45); **fig. 317**, *Pth.*, xxxiii., col. 6—red. JACOBY, *Rec. de Trav.*, xxi. 26,

would connect it with the napkin (?) held in hands of nobles.

⊔ two upright threads, the forked or looped ends crossed by two others: **fig. 311**, *Pth.*, xxxviii., under table. Cf. the varying figures in *Ä. T.*, Pl. 6-7 and 36, where different kinds of cloth are indicated by the different number of upright threads. Word-sign for *mnḫt*, "cloth."

*⊤ six upright threads, the forked or looped ends crossed by one horizontal thread from which hang other threads and an ⎰; **fig. 288**, *Pth.*, xxxviii. 4. Det. of *sšr*. Cf. the cloth ◂ *sšr* (?), one of the three kinds figured in very early tombs (*Medum*, xiii., &c.).

A symbol of cloth: **fig. 319**, *Akht.* Det. of *'nḫ* in offerings.

⎰ (*Hier.*, p. 46); *ntr*-roll of cloth: **fig. 324**, *Pth.*, xxxiii., col. 6—yellow, the lacing on the handle with alternate triangles of blue and green, and green bands.

⎰ (*Hier.*, p. 48); same compounded with bag: **fig. 307**, *Pth.*, xli. 6. In late times this was certainly used for *bd*, "natron (?)," and in early texts it appears to be det. to it, for some reason that is not very obvious. See DÜMICHEN, *Peduamenap*, i., Pl. xxii., no. 54, and L., *D.*, ii. 44. ⎰, ⎱ are misreadings of ⎰; and ⎰ (*Hier.*, p. 53) is a figment.

⎲ three upright threads with loops at side, looped thread across ends below: **fig. 304**, *Akht.* (cf. above fig. 252). Cf. MAR., *Mast.*, p. 492, with loops, while in *Methen*, L., *D.*, ii. 3, there are four toes showing the nails, evidently connected with the common value of the sign for *š'ḥ*, "toes" (LANGE, *Ä. Z.*, 1896, 77). Cf. 𒐰 = breadth of fingers (*Hier.*, pp. 45-6), usually only three. In late times, through linear hieratic, it becomes ⨅⨅.

linen running on cord, drawn together (?): **fig. 290**, *Pth.*, xxxii., col. 1, v. *Hier.*, p. 46, *s.v.*

(*Hier.*, p. 46); the same, spread out (?): **fig. 302**, *Pth.*, xxxii. 3.

Bag or purse: **fig. 312**, *Pth.*, xxxviii. 2; **fig. 318**, *ib.*, xxxvii., left, 2; **fig. 322**, *ib.*, xxxv., behind shoulder; **fig. 323**, *Akht.* White in L., D., ii. 96, *Ostseite*. In *Thy* it is carried by an attendant as a bag over his shoulder (N. de G. D.). Reading unknown. In *Kagemni* it stands for *šs* in amongst offerings.

spindle: **fig. 298**, *Akht.* Name, *mḥšf*, "spindle" (*Tdtb.*, cap. cliii.). Word-sign for *ḥšf*.

(*Hier.*, pp. 46-7); ball of string (?): **fig. 295** (green), *Pth.*, xxxiii., col. 9. In *Thy* this occurs as det. of *z'z't*, hence the circle O is probably the same as ⊚, and in that case ⊚ is det. of circle, in *qd*, "circle," &c.

O ball or disk: **fig. 289**, *Akht.* Det. of *qd* (see last).

(*Hier.*, p. 47); basket: **fig. 308**, *Pth.*, xxxiii., col. 9—green. Note its use as receptacle of sacred symbols, but only of feminine gender. The meaning of "holder" for the name of the basket is perhaps not justified, *nb* meaning "master," not "container."

(*Hier.*, p. 47); basket with loop: **fig. 309**, *Pth.*, xxxii., col. 3—green.

(*Hier.*, p. 47); reed mat or bundle as stool: **fig. 297**, *Pth.*, xxxix., col. 2—green.

(*Hier.*, p. 47); cake on mat: **fig. 303**, *Pth.*, xxxix., right, 3—mat green; in Akhethetep cake yellow, mat green. It probably represents a mat on which food would be placed, of which food the cake is the symbol; the modern correspondence would be a dish or plate. One name for food is *ḥtp't*, hence the word-sign value. *ḥtp* in all cases seems to mean "grace," or "favour," rather than "offering," or "gift."

possibly the tiller (?) of rudder oar (*ḥp't*): **fig. 292**, *Pth.*, xxxi. 3—green. Word-sign for *ḥp*.

bundle of stems (?) bound at middle and ends, often cut off slanting at top: **fig. 310**, *Pth.*, xxxi. 3—top slanting; **fig. 316**, *ib.*, xxxiii. 3—top straight. Cf. *Medum*, Pls. x., xii., xiii. Word-sign for *ys't*, in "labourers," "crew of ship"; see *Dend.*, Pl. xiii., tomb 331, for the rare full spelling; also in (cf. *Medum*, Pl. 10), *Pyr.*, T. 87 = N., 618—in title, *šmšw ys't*. When used for , the spelling is full , indicating that this is the derived value, and that *ys't* is the original. The origin of its presumed name or pictorial value, *ys't*, is not clear.

bundle of short stems tied by rope: **fig. 314**, *Pth.*, xxxiv., col. 2; **fig. 321**, *Pth.*, xxxii., col. 4; in *Akht.*, green. Word-sign and phon. for , meaning "boundary," "complete," &c. Cf. *Sanehat*, l. 198, "wrapping of dead (?)."

(*Hier.*, p. 43); hank of fibres: **fig. 313**, *Pth.*, xxxii., before head—green.

(*Hier.*, p. 43); coil of rope: **fig. 289**, *Akht.*, det. of *q's*; **fig. 301**, *Pth.*, xxxi. 5, first to right, numeral 100. The second value in *Hier.* should be ⟶ (not ⟶); it seems to have led confusedly to a later value, *šn*. Cf. SPIEGELBERG, Ä. Z., 1898, 138.

⌀ (*Hier.*, p. 44); cord on stick: **fig. 296,** *Pth.*, xxxiii., col. 3.

⅄ (*Hier.*, p. 44); girdle (?): **fig. 315,** *Pth.*, xxxiv., top. J. H. WALKER suggests that this is probably a girdle rope, with slip-knot to fasten apron round waist. On coffins it is associated as much with waist-cloths and aprons as with weapons.

⅀ (*Hier.*, p. 45); cord, possibly gathered up for throwing ("far"?, cf. *w'*, "far"), as in the bola: **fig. 306,** *Pth.*, xxxi. 2.

Ω (*Hier.*, p. 45); loop of cord, ends downwards: **fig. 293,** *Pth.*, xli. 2; **fig. 300,** *Akht.*

ᚨ loop of cord, ends upward: **fig. 291,** *Pth.*, xxxii. 2—yellow in Akhethetep. Name, *šš*, "cord" (*Pth.*, *l.c.*). Phon. for *šš*. In late writing det. of clothing, &c.

⟼ (*Hier.*, p. 45); cord handle: **fig. 294,** *Pth.*, xxxii. 3.

⫰⫰⫰ (*Hier.*, p. 45); many-looped rope knot: **fig. 299,** *Pth.*, xxxii. 3.

ᚩ yoke (?): **fig. 305,** *Pth.*, xxxi. 3. Cf. *Medum*, Pl. ix. (also xxiv.), which indicates that the cross-piece is of wood, the hoop of twisted rope or rushes (?). An object difficult to recognize, but probably connected with cattle. It seems to mean "stable," "stall," "cattle-shed." Name, 𓄿𓏏 *mz·t*. Word-sign for 𓄿𓏏. It may represent a large basket, over-turned and empty, but with the pole for carrying it, and perhaps called *mz·t*, "the deep." Probably identical with the sign ᚩ, which signifies the corn-measure *h'r* (*Kah. Pap.*, xxii., 14, 16), and which is det. of all kinds of basket-work, litters, chairs, &c. The uses of this sign need to be well studied, and its relation to allied forms determined.

CLASS XIII. INSTRUMENTS OF WAR, HUNTING, &c. PL. XV.

⌒ (*Hier.*, p. 51); bow or yoke: **fig. 338,** *Akht.*

⟼ (*Hier.*, p. 51): arrow: **fig. 326,** *Akht.*

⎐ (*Hier.*, p. 51); mace: **fig. 330,** *Pth.*, xxxiii., col. 7—handle yellow. Phon. in *phz*, *Pap. Eb.*

⎞ (*Hier.*, p. 51); boomerang of the fowling type: **fig. 328,** *Pth.*, xli. 19; **fig. 329,** *ib.*, 9. *qm'* means "throw" (LEFÉBURE, *Sphinx*, iii. 88.

◁ cleaver head, or blade of *w'*-harpoon: **fig. 337,** *Akht.* = fig. 407 coloured blue. Cf. *Una*, l. 14. Nome-sign of XXIInd nome of Upper Egypt (Aphroditopolite); later written with ◥. As J. de Rougé pointed out, *Piankhy*, l. 145, gives the name of this nome 𓃀𓏤𓎡𓃀⊗ *mtnr*. Hence ◁ is probably the "axe-head" or "cleaver" 𓌪𓏤𓏤𓂻 *mtny·t* (*Mentuhotep*, p. 27, no. 8); and being made of metal, it is perhaps the early form of a sign for copper (ᗡ in the XVIIIth Dyn.), which may, perhaps, read *ḥmti* (?), as the origin of the Coptic ϩⲟⲙⲧ.

⎗ dagger in sheath (?): **fig. 334,** *Pth.*, xxxix. l. 2. In *Medum*, Pl. xiii., red blade or sheath, white handle (ivory?); in L., *D.*, ii. 96, *Ostseite*, all blue. Its upper part resembles the peg to which the cord of the net is attached in the fowling scene in *Pth.*, xxxii. 3; but a dagger in *Mentuhotep*, Pl. v., and p. 29, no. 31, is named 𓊪, meaning, perhaps, "first quality." Word-sign for *tpi*, "chief," *tp.*

⁕ ⟼ boat on water: **fig. 331,** *Pth.*, xxxi., col. 4—boat green. Det. of *q'q'*, "barge," and of boats in general in O.K. It may be picture word-sign for *q'q'* (cf. ERM., *Westcar*, viii. 2), or for *ymw*, "boat" (being in the basse-époque a common word-sign for *ym*). Sometimes = *w'y*, "boat" (generally a mythological boat, and the form of the sign generally modified accordingly).

(*Hier.*, p. 52); fisherman's boat, containing net, on water: **fig. 336**, *Akht.*

(*Hier.*, p. 52); paddle: **fig. 332**, *Pth.*, xxxix., left, 3.

(*Hier.*, p. 52); bone harpoon-head: **fig. 333**, *Pth.*, xxxii. 4; **fig. 339**, *Akht.* (Note that in *Hier.*, p. 53, and are both base or false, founded respectively on and .)

Harpoon (*w'*, *Hier.*, p. 52) on stand in a boat with tow-line (?) (cf. bark of Sokaris, &c.), the whole placed on a sacred perch: **fig. 327**, *Pth.*, xxxiv. 1. Symbol of the VIIth nome of Lower Egypt (in the Western Delta), and of the VIIIth (in the Eastern Delta), the Heroopolite. Reading unknown. Cf. *Methen*, L., *D.*, ii. 3, top right.

(*Hier.*, p. 53); bird-trap: **fig. 335**, *Pth.*, xxxii. 3.

cage or crate for birds: **fig. 325**, *Pth.*, xxxii. 3. Det. and word-sign for name, "box."

CLASS XIV. ARTICLES FOR PERSONAL USE, FURNITURE, FOOD, &c. PL. XV.

(*Hier.*, p. 54); conventionalized throne: **fig. 352**, *Pth.*, xxxiii., col. 6—blue or green. Where in Ptahhetep the sign is repeated in a row, it is in alternating colours (*Pth.*, xli., cols. 2, 3).

coffin: **fig. 340**, *Pth.*, xxxix., left, 1, Name, *hn.* Det. *qrs't*, "burial." Cf. , *Hier.*, p. 54.

Food-stand (*Hier.*, p. 54): **fig. 345**, *Akht.* Det. of *h't.* Cf. *Medum*, Pl. xiii. In *Pth.*, xli. 15 has food only, no vases as in M.K.

the same, with slices of bread (cf. *Hier.*, p. 54): **fig. 346**, *Akht.* For the variety with palm leaves, which seems to belong chiefly to the period of debasement at the end of the O.K., see *Dendereh*, pp. 42, 53.

(*Hier.*, p. 55); loaf of bread: **fig. 351**, *Akht.*

flat circular cake or dish, marks at the edge, in some cases evidently the impress of three or four fingers: **fig. 350**, *Pth.*, xxxix., l. 2; also *ib.*, xli., offerings, 16; **fig. 402**, coloured, where two grains are shown on the top. A det. of offerings. Word-sign for *p't* (?).

a *wšḥ*-vase piled with food: **fig. 348**, *Pth.*, xxxvi. 2; **fig. 349**, *ib.*, xli., offerings, 20—contents green (?). Det. of *rnp't*, "vegetable (?)."

(*Hier.*, p. 55); staff: **fig. 344**, *Pth.*, xxxiii., col. 8. N.B. The short staves of the ox-herds (*ib.*, xxxi.) are not much longer in proportion. Yellow in Akhethetep.

(*Hier.*, p. 55); **fig. 342**, *Akht.*; fig. 408 (coloured), *Akht.* In *Pth.* the pot is blue, the stick red with the middle black. The pencase is partly covered with black leather, forming a holder for the pens. For the value see SETHE, *Verbum*, i., § 260. SETHE prefers to interpret this spelling as for *sš*, on the strength of the Coptic equivalent, though the spelling *sš* is found even in N.K.

(*Hier.*, p. 55); papyrus-roll: **fig. 310**, *Pth.*, xxxi., col. 2; in Akhethetep seal blue, green in one example. Note that is not *š't*, but *mz't*, "book," or "roll," fully written in *Pyr. W.*, l. 601, and this value is transferred in *mz'·t*, "chisel," as was first pointed out by BRUGSCH, *v. P. S. B. A.*, 1899, 269-70. Its use in *Pth.* is restricted, as generally in the O.K.; it is word-sign for ―――, xxxiii. 6, and det. to (*ird*) *mdw*, "order," xxxi.-xxxiii., cols. 3, 4, and to "tribute" (registered).

―――― (*Hier.*, p. 56); draught-board with men: **fig. 343**, *Pth.*, xxxii. 2; **fig. 347**, *ib.*, xli. col. 2. The board is generally green with black lines, sometimes red with black lines; the smaller men are generally green. The number of divisions is usually 3 × 11, but sometimes 3 × 12 or 13.

CLASS XV. INSIGNIA, SYMBOLS, &c. PL. XVI.

(*Hier.*, p. 57); crook sceptre: **fig. 358**, *Pth.*, xxxi. 3.

(*Hier.*, p. 57); mallet (?)-symbol: **fig. 362**, *Pth.*, xxxix., left, 2—blue. Cf. BORCHARDT, *Ä. Z.*, 1899, p. 82, for additional evidence that it is a mallet, the value *ḥn* being connected with a word *ḥn* used of beating with a mallet.

(*Hier.*, p. 57); *sekhem*-sceptre: **fig. 360**, *Pth.*, xxxi., col. 4. It is adorned with many bands of colour, which in Akhethetep seem to be blue, red, blue, green, with green papyrus head. The reading *ḥrp* still requires further proof; it is at any rate confined to titles. One may compare (*El. B.*, I., xiv., l. 3), corresponding to the title (*Kah. Pap.*, xv. 15, &c.). In (quoted *Hier.*, p. 58) *ḥrp* is verb in infinitive rather than a title.

(*Hier.*, p. 58); cylinder seal: **fig. 354**, *Akht.*, with curved loop; **fig. 356**, *Pth.*, xxxiii. 3, with upright loop. In another example in Ptahhetep the knot is blue, also the central band of the cylinder; the rest of the cylinder is apparently red.

(*Hier.*, p. 58); *user*-sceptre: **fig. 361**, *Pth.*, xxxiii. 7.

(*Hier.*, p. 59); *was*-sceptre (with head of Set-animal (?), MASPERO) with loop at top, as name of Thebes: **fig. 257**. Demotic variants (*Rhind bil.*, no. 417) show that its root terminated with *s*, and its confusion with *ws(r)* in demotic shows that it read approximately *ws*: thus it evidently has the same value as *w's*, with the fem. ending, and the name of the city and nome was *W's·t*. Cf. also the spelling on a stela of the XXth Dyn. in SETHE, *Verbum*, i. 142.

(*Hier.*, p. 59); *ded* pillar: **fig. 359**, *Pth.*, xxxix., right, 1. The stem is in painted bands, red and green alternating (?).

(*Hier.*, p. 60); *'nḫ* girdle-knot: **fig. 355**, *Pth.*, xxxii. 4; in Akhethetep blue.

s'-loop: **fig. 353**, *Pth.*, xxxviii. 1. Varies with (*Hier.*, p. 45); rare in O.K. except in proper names and cartouches. It is apparently part of the outfit of marsh men, carried on stick over shoulder in Akht. An early bronze amulet of this form is figured in *El Kab*, Pl. v. 5.

UNCLASSIFIED. PL. XVII.

(*Hier.*, p. 56); flute (?), wooden wedge (?), cubit-rod (?): **fig. 393**, *Pth.*, xxxiii., col. 3—tapering; **fig. 394**, *ib.*, xxxix., left, 2—rounded edge; **fig. 395**, *Akht.*—rectangular. Nearly always slightly tapering in Ptahhetep. If this represents a wedge in different aspects it would imply "straightening," "adjusting."

☥ (*Hier.*, p. 61); **fig. 376**, *Pth.*, xxxiii., col. 5—red centre in Akhethetep. Word-sign for *nz*.

⚱ (*Hier.*, p. 61); **fig. 383**, *Pth.*, xxxiv. 4. Word-sign for *śn*.

⟵ (*Hier.*, p. 53); **fig. 380**, *Pth.*, xli., offerings, 22. Word-sign for *rtḥ*.

⚖ supposed to be connected with a balance, or special kind of cutting tool (?): **fig. 387**, *Akht.*—all red. Word-sign for *wẕʿ*, "dissever," "divide," "judge," "weigh."

Drill (?): **fig. 384**, *Akht.* Read *wbʾ*. MAX MÜLLER, *Rec. de Trav.*, ix. 162, the first to fix the readings of this and a number of similar signs, thought it distinct from •ꝯ, which is a hand-drill for hollowing out stone vessels, weighted and steadied by two stones at the top (BORCHARDT, *Ä. Z.*, 1897, 107). The Egyptians seem to have considered this as a symbol of mechanical skill, and its word-sign value is *ḥm* in *ḥm·t*, "craft," *ḥm·ti*, "craftsmen." *wbʾ*, to "bore," "pierce," is probably sometimes spelt with •ꝯ, and fig. 384 represents, perhaps, some similar instrument for the same purpose, such as a bow-drill; in *Pyr. P.*, 174, a string crosses the stock. The circular object below may be intended to represent the hole drilled.

ꝯ (*Hier.*, p. 62); symbol for "attendant": **fig. 379**, *Pth.*, xxxiii. 6, a fine example, indicating the man called Nefer-renpet. The loop which is sometimes found at the top of this sign in the E.R.A. volume is erroneous. The knife (?) is doubtful. The reading *šms*, rather than *ŝs*, is confirmed by two good instances in DARESSY, *Rec. de Trav.*, xiv. 21; quoted by PIEHL, who considers the other examples insufficient to establish the reading as being possibly due to error. CAPART, *Ä. Z.*, 1898, p. 125, has a note on this sign, but his argument

requires more support. In N.K. the sign is used in curious combinations, which have probably little pictorial meaning.

⟋ (*Hier.*, p. 62); whip (?): **fig. 371**, *Pth.*, xxxi. 2; **fig. 372**, *Akht.*; **fig. 377**, *Pth.*, xxxviii. 1—in name 🦅🦊, green with black lines. Differs from figures of whips in the scenes only by the projecting end above the lash (?); this detail seems invariably present in the hieroglyph.

A conventional figure, apparently for mud, dung: **fig. 385**, *Pth.*, xxxii. 2—brown. Det. of *sp*, "caulk," with clay (?). Word-sign for *ḥs*, "dung," with this usage more realistically represented in *Pyr.* Det. of evil-smelling things, decay, &c., *syn*, "rot." In *Pth.*, xxxiii. (see Pl. iii. of present volume), the word *mḥsḥs* should be restored, determined by a man with this sign in his hand, a det. to which fig. 385 alone corresponds in Thy (see *Hier.*, p. 63, *s.v.* ◯). ◯ *ḥsb* seems distinct from this *ḥs* in hieratic throughout, though in hieroglyphs confused with it.

🪜 (*Hier.*, p. 63); *ḥr*-stand: **fig. 363**, *Pth.*, xxxviii., near head; **fig. 365**, *ib.*, xxxiii. 6—black with red in middle; **fig. 370**, *Akht.*; **fig. 374**, *Pth.*, xxxix., over canopy.

⛏ (*Hier.*, p. 64); **fig. 366**, *Pth.*, xxxix., right, 1.

Granary: **fig. 369**, *Akht.*; **fig. 373**, *Pth.*, xxxv. 5; **fig. 378**, *Pth.*, xxxi. 3; **fig. 401**, *Akht.*—coloured black and blue. Cf. *Medum*, Pl. xx., offerings, where similar figures have the names of cereals upon them. Word-sign for *šnwt*, "corn-store" (*Pyr. P.*, 395; *N.*, 1170). Later its form resembles a heap of grain on a floor.

⟋ possibly one side of the whiskers of man

or animal: **fig. 380**, *Pth.*, xli. 5 (= *ym*); **fig. 381**, *Akht.*—coloured red; **fig. 382**, *Pth.*, xxxiii. 5 (= *ym*, as is shown by the parallel in Mera). Red in L., *D.*, ii. 70. After M.K. it takes the form ⌒. Word-sign for *gš*, "side," "half," and phon. Word-sign for *ym*, "side (?)" (*Pth.*, xxxiii. 5 = *Mera*, p. 551), and phon. In N.K. very common as alph. for *m*. Cf. CALICE, *Ä. Z.*, 1897, 170.

*Å (*Hier.*, p. 47); **fig. 391**, *Pth.*, xxxii. 3. Apparently word-sign for *zb'*. Mr. Davies observes that it is almost identical in form with the floats or tassels (?) attached to the harpoon in a scene of hunting the hippopotamus in the tomb of Mera.

*⌒ apparently an ornamental tassel, like the *mnh't* of *Mentuhotep*, Pl. iii., and p. 20, no. 27: **fig. 397**, *Akht.* Phon. for *zb'* or *'pr*. Such ornaments seem to have been called ⌐ □ ⌒; hence one value of the sign.

∩ hoop of wood or metal (?): **fig. 396**, *Pth.*, xxxi. 4. Word-sign for 10; in Coptic ⲙⲏⲧ, ⲙⲉⲧ. In a very late text written ⌐∩ *mt*. For the form cf. the hoop in the ground (Pl. xvii.). PETRIE, *Medum*, p. 33, notes the resemblance to ⋔ (see above, p. 33). SETHE, *Ä. Z.*, 1896, 90, considers it essentially the same as ⋔, and would give 𓄿 *mz* as its original value. Judging from Coptic, the multiples of 10 from 50 to 90 were formed as a kind of plural of the units 5 to 9, but 20, 30, 40 had distinct names, of which 𓄿 ⌐□ 𓄿 𓄿 , for ∩∩∩, 30, alone is known. By phon. trans. ∩∩∩ is word-sign for a kind of spear.

Stone covered by cloth (?): **fig. 367**, *Pth.*, xxxix. 2. Occurs in O.K. as det. of the festival of *w'g*, and more rarely of that of *zhrt't*, perhaps as representing a place for offerings.

⌣ (*Hier.*, p. 64); **fig. 364**, *Pth.*, xxxii. 3.

Occurs with ⌂ as det. of *hb*, "festival," none of the usual detail being shown. In Pl. xxxviii. the hieroglyph occurs on a vase in the hand of Ptahhetep. Here it shows oblique striping.

◊ unguent vase upside down, alabaster markings: **fig. 392**, *Akht.* Some early M.K. examples substitute for this a mirror in its case (*v.* BORCHARDT, *Ä. Z.*, 1897, 116. In O.K. variant *škr* for ⌐○⌒, meaning "adorner" or "adornment" as title of woman (SPIEGELBERG, *Ä. Z.*, 1896, 162).

{ (*Hier.*, p. 26, *s.v.* }): **fig. 388**, *Pth.*, xxxiii. 6.

{ (*Hier.*, p. 26, *s.v.* }): **fig. 390**, *Pth.*, xli. 20.

⊗ **fig. 368**, *Pth.*, xxxiv., top, 4; cf. *Medum*, Pl. xxviii. Word-sign for Hieraconpolis, *Nhn*; cf. late variants in BR., *D. G.*, 353, 1227. Early variants (*Ä. Z.*, 1890, 69) show only that the name ended with *n*. Colour and form suggest the snout of a pig or the end of an elephant's proboscis as the origin of this sign.

⌒ **fig. 389**, *Pth.*, xxxi. 2—coloured green. It occurs over ⌐⌐ amongst roughly-cut hieroglyphs, where one would expect ⩶, but the colour and all is wrong for ⌒. MASPERO, *Ét. Ég.*, ii. 209, note 5, suggested that it might be intended for *wdb* (cf. fig. 219).

◊ (*v.* ◊, *Hier.*, p. 50); blade of knife: **fig. 386**, *Pth.*, xli. 22 (in *nms't*). Colourless in L., *D.*, ii. 70.

MISCELLANEOUS DETAILS ON PLATE XVI.

In the centre is a cartouche of Ne-user-Ra (Pl. xxxiii., col. 7).

On the left the shell hung from the neck of the ox in Pl. xxxi. 3; a tether for a calf, Pl. xxxi. 1; and a milking-jar from *Akht.*, as it appears in a milking scene, with either a leaf in the mouth or the steam rising from it. The milk-vase usually has some such object in the mouth (*Hieroglyphs*, p. 40, where the idea of a feeder is probably wrong).

On the right, the amulet worn by Ptah-hetep (Pl. xxxi.), dark colour; bull from the nome-sign before the third figure in Pl. xxxiv. 1; servant with offerings, Pl. xxxvii., bottom right.

APPENDIX.

NOTES TO THE PLATES PUBLISHED BY THE EGYPTIAN RESEARCH ACCOUNT.

PLATE XXXI.

Heading.—Correct this to **E. WALL: S. HALF.**[2]

Reg. 1*a*.—For ▢ read 〚. After ✚ insert the determinative. (See Corrections to Plates, p. 42.)

Reg. 1*b*.—A man is kneeling below the cow on the extreme left, and is milking her. The calving cow is stretching up her head so that her long horn extends into the register above. Below the ⌒ in front of her add ⌒ (⌒?). For a remnant of the next legend see drawing, p. 42.

The herdsmen have their hands in the mouths of the recumbent cattle (to feed them?).

The removal of a stone has caused the loss of the superscription. It began with ⌁ apparently.

Reg. 2.—Under the ⫻ is an ♀ in paint.

The lines of the shoulder and chest of the last two oxen have been confused (see Pl. xxvii.).

Before the third figure is a painted inscription (see p. 42).

The last herdsman wears the projecting tunic, the sculptor having corrected his first line, which is the one followed by the copyists.

Reg. 3.—For the shape of ⫯ see fig. 310.

---

[1] The numbering of the columns follows the reading. The registers are numbered from the top. The photographs (Pls. xxiii.—xxx.) should be consulted in connexion with these notes, and the key plans on Plates ii. and xxi. will help the reader to realize the relative position of the scenes. The drawings shown on p. 42 are only in a few instances strict facsimiles or drawn to an exact scale.

[2] The walls are already correctly named in Mr. Griffith's Introduction to the publication.

For the name (in paint) of the leader of the second ox see p. 42.

Reg. 4*b*.—The number of ducks would seem to be 100,002; see p. 42.

Ptahhetep's staff should have the usual rounded head. For the true shape of his amulet see Pl. xvi.

PLATE XXXII.

Heading.—Correct this to **E. WALL: N. HALF.**

Col. 1.—Read at end ⌒ ⌁.

Reg. 1.—For bushes painted on the background and title of hunter see Pl. xxii.

Reg. 3.—For the form of *zb'* see fig. 391.

For the half-cut determinative of *ḥn* see facsimile, p. 42.

The name of the man putting fowl in the cage is Chnemhetep, the vase being painted only.

Reg. 3*b*.—The *ḥb* should be of the shape of fig. 247.

PLATE XXXIII. (upper half).

Title.—Correct this to **E. WALL, TOP: S. HALF.**

Col. 4.—See p. 42.

Col. 5.—See p. 42.

Reg. 1.—For the correct posture of the arms of the first and third youths see the photograph, Pl. xxiv.*b*.

The name Akhethetep occurs before the second group of wrestlers as well.

Reg. 2.—Prefix *sḥz* to the title of Seshemnefer.

The tie of the huntsman's dress and of the dogs' collars is green. He wears sandals. The little dog has a curling tail.

The 𓊪 should in every case be shaped as in fig. 379.

PLATE XXXIII. (lower half).

Title.—Correct this to **E. WALL, TOP: N. HALF.**

Cols. 2, 3, 4.—After 𓄿 ⟨⟩ ⊗ read △.

In all pyramid signs there should be a horizontal line near the apex, as in fig. 246.

Reg. 1.—The cord passes round the bundle of papyrus, which is between the fifth and sixth figures, and then round the shoulders of both of them. Owing to the bad light near the ceiling and the worn stone, a part of the scene was thought by the copyists to be destroyed. It will be found on Pl. iii.

Reg. 2.—Read 𓂝 beneath the arrow of *st.* Both youths have darts in each hand.

The second legend ends in □ ⌇⌇⌇ ⎯𓂝𓂝, followed apparently by another sign. The band across the breast of the striding lad is blue.

The first sign over the boy who is being assaulted is ⌐𝄇. The inscription above ends 𓍿 ⌇⌇⌇ ⌇⌇⌇ ⟨⟩ ⟨⟩ ⟨⟩.

The figures in this register show by their yellow flesh-colour, their side-lock, and their uncircumcised state that they are all young lads. They wear round their necks either a narrow circlet with a green centre-stone, a broad green collar, or a pendant necklace, to which a blue amulet shaped like that of Ptah-hetep (Pl. xvi.) is attached. (These details are in paint only.)

Reg. 3.—The second figure has the title 𓏏𓏤𓏤𓏤𓏤𓏤𓏤𓏤𓏤.

The fourth is called ⟨⟩ 𓂝 𓏤.

The wine wrung out is painted blue. The mass that is being trodden out is blue, with darker spots to represent the berries. The vine

is coloured as in fig. 405. Blue water is being poured from a red pot.

PLATE XXXIV.

Heading.—Correct this to **S. WALL.**

Columns.—Pieces of the broken wall, sufficient to supply the lacuna, have been recovered (see Pl. iii.). Col. 1 plainly ended with *stn.*

Reg. 1.—The name of the first figure should end with ⊗.

For more complete copies of the second and fourth nome-signs see figs. 327 and 22.

Before the third figure was one of the nome-signs containing the bull. For this (recovered from the *débris*) see Pl. xvi.

The lines of the women's dress have been somewhat confused. All should have a tress of the wig hanging over the bosom, the two shoulder straps, and the necklace (as in Pl. xxxv.).

Reg. 2.—The | after 𓂝 should be plain.

The slaughterers carry the usual knife-sharpener, stuck inside their belts behind, and attached to the front of the belt by a cord. The knives are set in backs, apparently. For this, and for the names and titles of the first and third figures, see p. 42.

Reg. 3.—Cancel the base line under the figures determinative of 𓏤, and insert one between this register and the next below.

Correct the names of the second and fifth figures to ⟨⟩ 𓏤𓏤 □ and 𓄿 ⟨⟩ 𓂝 (i.e. fig. 322).

PLATE XXXV. (upper half).

Title.—Alter this to **S. WALL, TOP.**

Columns.—Read 𓏤𓂝. For completion of lower part see Pl. iii.

Reg. 2.—Before the fourth figure read 𓆓 𓂝. In place of the blank enclosures before the last two figures are inscriptions in faded ink. For the apparent reading see approximate sketch on p. 42. The first, third, and fourth figures (as also the last figure in Reg. 3) have green pads on their heads like the eighth. Some of the baskets are finely woven in green and yellow wicker-work.

PLATE XXXV. (lower half).

Title.—Alter this to **N. WALL, TOP.**
The name of the servant with the box behind **Ptahhetep** is ⟨hieroglyphs⟩; that of the attendant **touch**ing Ptahhetep's face is ⟨hieroglyphs⟩(?) ⟨hieroglyphs⟩.

. Reg. 1.—For the title of the two musicians see fig. 35. The harps seem to rest, or to be fixed, on a flat base furnished with a back piece, which a stay supports. A couchant figure of a lion forms an ornamental foot to this stand.

Each end of the first collar represents the head of a hawk. The dwarfs on the left hand have one hand raised, and hold a collar somewhat similar to the first.

Reg. 2.—The ⟨hieroglyph⟩ (fourth title) should be of the usual shape.

Read ⟨hieroglyph⟩ (fifth name).

Reg. 3.—The second figure is named ⟨hieroglyphs⟩.

Reg. 4.—The name of the boy (yellow flesh-tint) at Ptahhetep's feet is ⟨hieroglyphs⟩.

PLATE XXXVI.

Heading.—Correct this to **N. WALL, LOWER HALF.**
The first and second registers should change places.

Reg. 1 (properly Reg. 2).—Read ⟨hieroglyphs⟩.

The title over shoulder of first figure is ⟨hieroglyph⟩; the name of the sixth ⟨hieroglyphs⟩; in that of the fourth delete ⟨hieroglyph⟩.

The other hands of the last two figures appear grasping the stem of the stand.

Reg. 2 (properly Reg. 1).—Read ⟨hieroglyphs⟩.

For more accurate forms of first, second, fifth, and sixth names see next page.

Reg. 3.—For the form of ⟨hieroglyph⟩ see fig. 155.

Reg. 4.—The left-hand ox is coloured grey with large blue-black spots. The bowl and the heart (hung on the little finger) are red.

PLATE XXXVII.

The scenes face inward. The left-hand column, therefore, is taken from the left (E.) side of the doorway as one enters, the other from the right (W.).

Reg. 1 (E.).—For slight additions on the east side see Pl. iii.

Reg. 2 (W.).—For the names see next page.

Reg. 3 (W.).—The fourth name is ⟨hieroglyphs⟩.

Reg. 4 (W.).—For the fourth servant see Pl. xvi. On the E. wall there are traces of names.

PLATE XXXVIII.

Heading. — Correct this to **W. WALL, CENTRE.**

Reg. 1.—The first name is ⟨hieroglyphs⟩ (see fig. 377).

Reg. 2.—Read ⟨hieroglyphs⟩ (i.e. fig. 322).

Reg. 3. — Over the last servant read ⟨hieroglyphs⟩.

Reg. 4.—The first ḥr ḥb should have a sash across the breast.

For the sšr sign see fig. 288.

PLATE XXXIX.

Heading.—Correct this to **W. WALL, S. FALSE DOOR.**

Col. 1 (numbering from the right).—For the form of the qrrt sign here and in col. 8 see fig. 242.

For the form of bya and ḥr ntr signs see figs. 195 and 87.

Col. 4.—⊗ should have the cross-lines and ⊙ the central spot.

Col. 7.—Read ▢ 𓅨 .

PLATE XL.

Heading.—Correct this to **W. WALL, N. DOOR** (see Pls. xix. and xx.).

PLATE XLI.

Title.—Correct this to **SCALE 1:8. W. WALL, CENTRE.**

Columns.—For the pyramid signs see fig. 246 ; for ⎓ (col. 4) see fig. 218.

Col. 1 (of offerings, numbering from the left). The determinative in reg. 1 is a man pouring liquid from a vase. For the animal in reg. 3 see fig. 74.

Col. 3.—Read ⌢ 𓄑 𓐖 .

Col. 9.—See below.

Cols. 11 and 12.—For ⚬⚬ see fig. 147.

Col. 13, reg. 2.—Read ⌢ 𓅨 (a ?, not *tyw*).

Col. 14, reg. 1.—See below.

Col. 16, reg. 1.—Read ⎀ ⌢ . Reg. 2.—The determining figure carries three pellets on his arm. Reg. 3.—Delete the first ⌢.

Col. 18, reg. 1.—The *ḥm* sign is shaped as in fig. 195. The figure should hold nothing in his hand. Reg. 3.—Read 𓁐 𓈖 .

Col. 19.—For the *bnr* sign see fig. 184.

Col. 22, reg. 2.—Read 𓅨 ⎓

Col. 23.—The first sign should be *nm* (fig. 386). Reg. 2.—The onions should lie on a basket (fig. 175).

Col. 24, reg. 2.—For the *ḫpsh* sign see fig. 140.

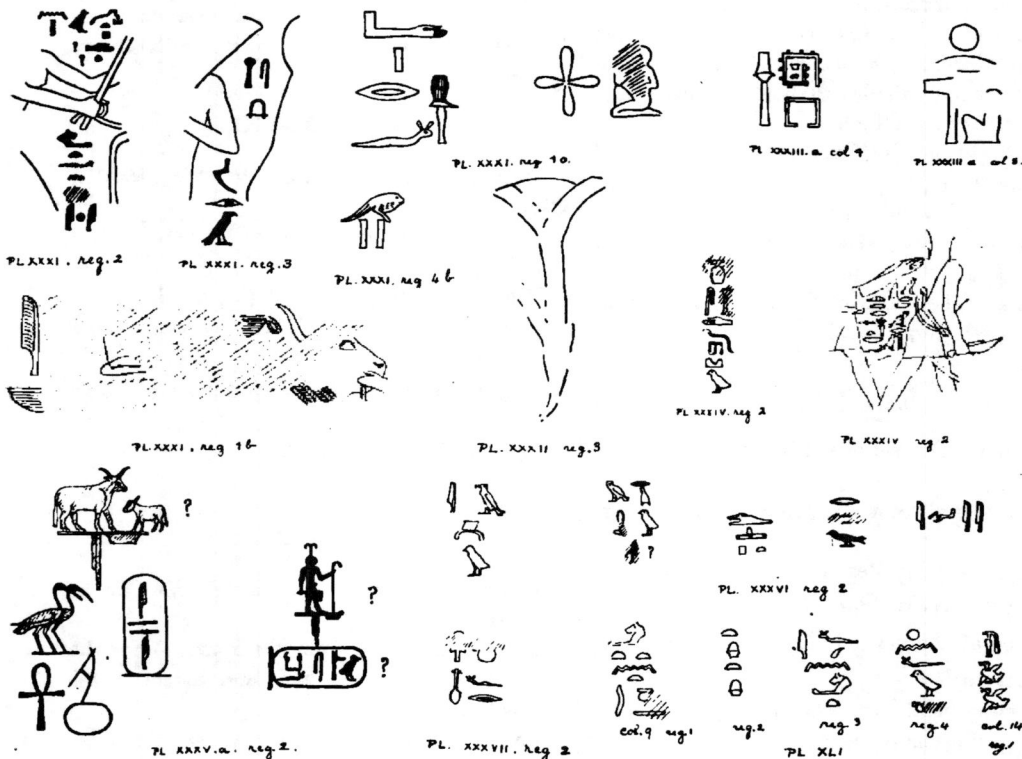

CORRECTIONS TO PLATES.

PLATES.

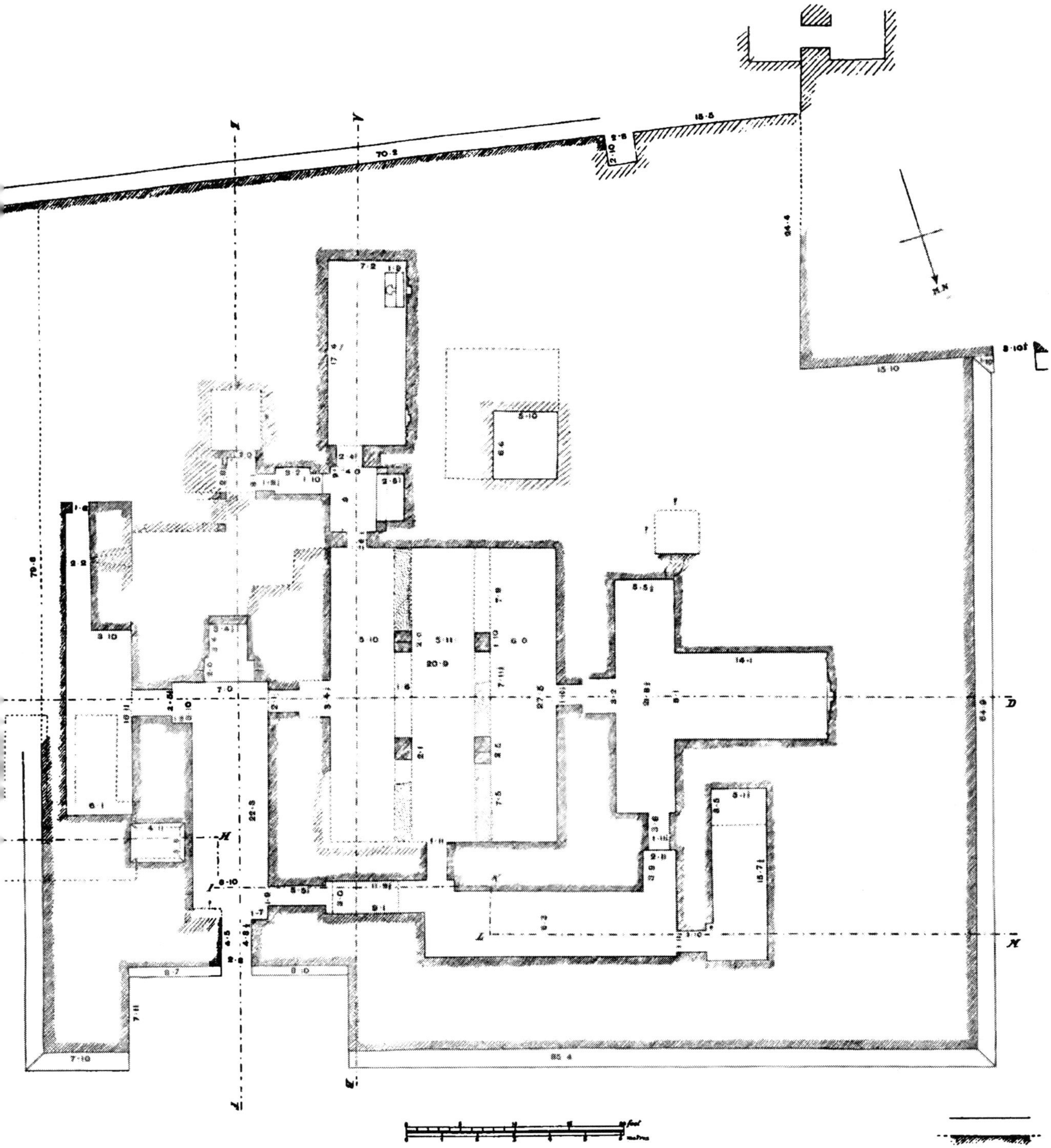

Plate II.

SECTION OF MASTABA, Etc.

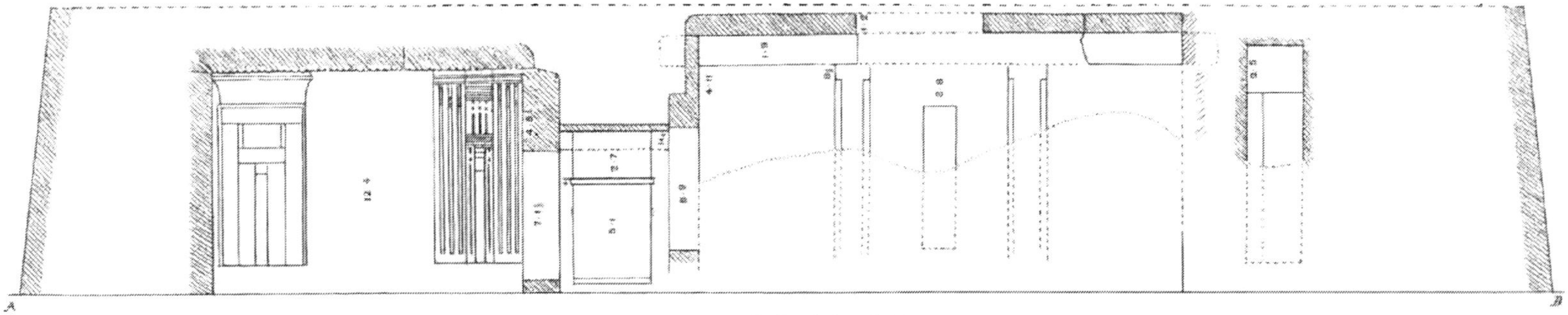
A
B
12·4

SECTION ON A.B. *(Scale ⅛ inch to the foot).*

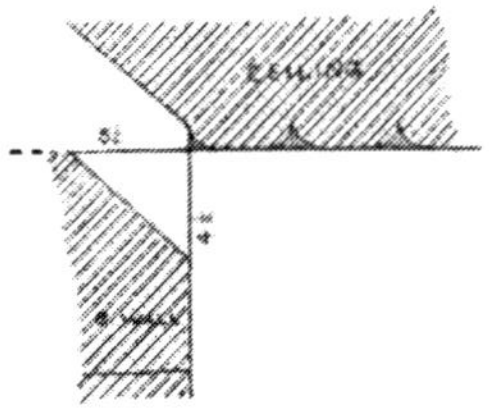

AIR PASSAGE

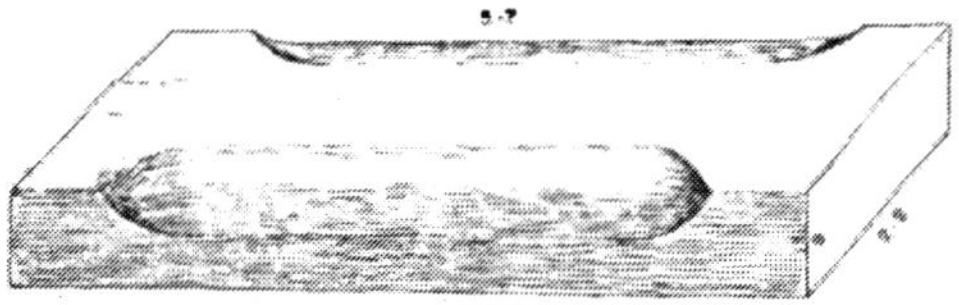
5·7

LID OF A SARCOPHAGUS

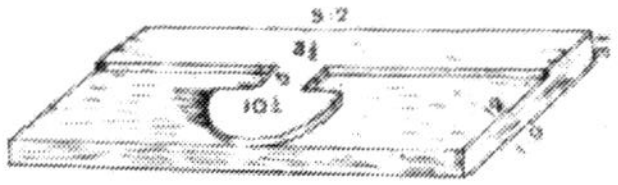
3·2

TABLE OF OFFERINGS

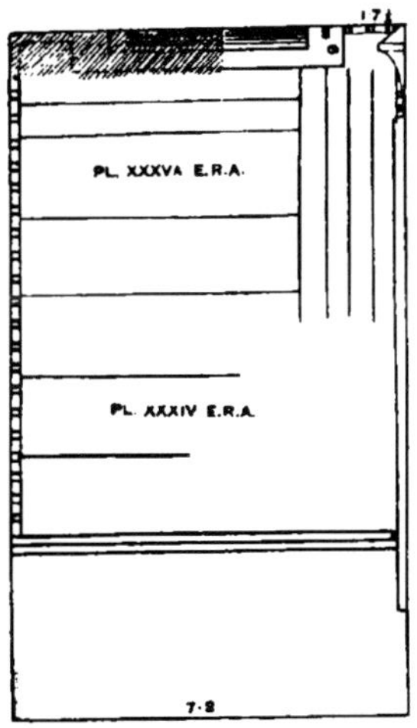
PL. XXXVA E.R.A.
PL. XXXIV E.R.A.
7·2

S. WALL

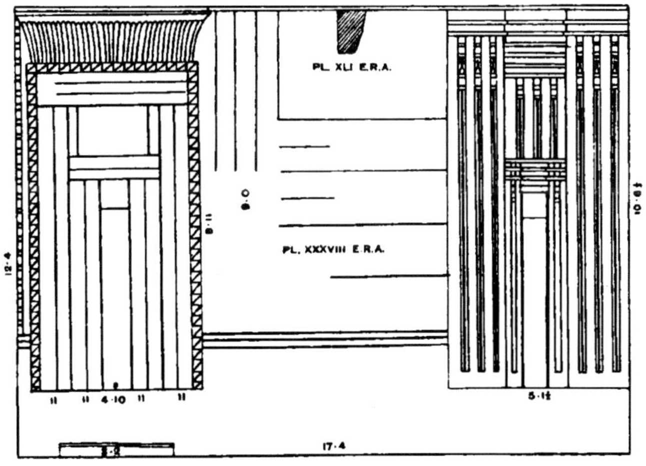
PL. XLI E.R.A.
PL. XXXVIII E.R.A.
12·4
10·6½
5·1½
17·4

W. WALL

(Scale ¼ in. to the foot)

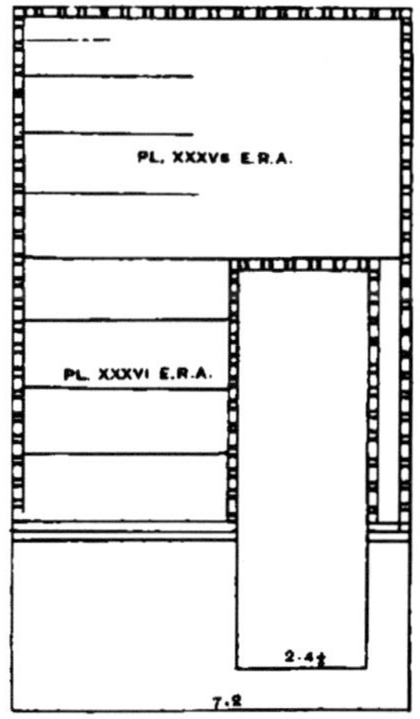
PL. XXXVB E.R.A.
PL. XXXVI E.R.A.
2·4½
7·2

N. WALL

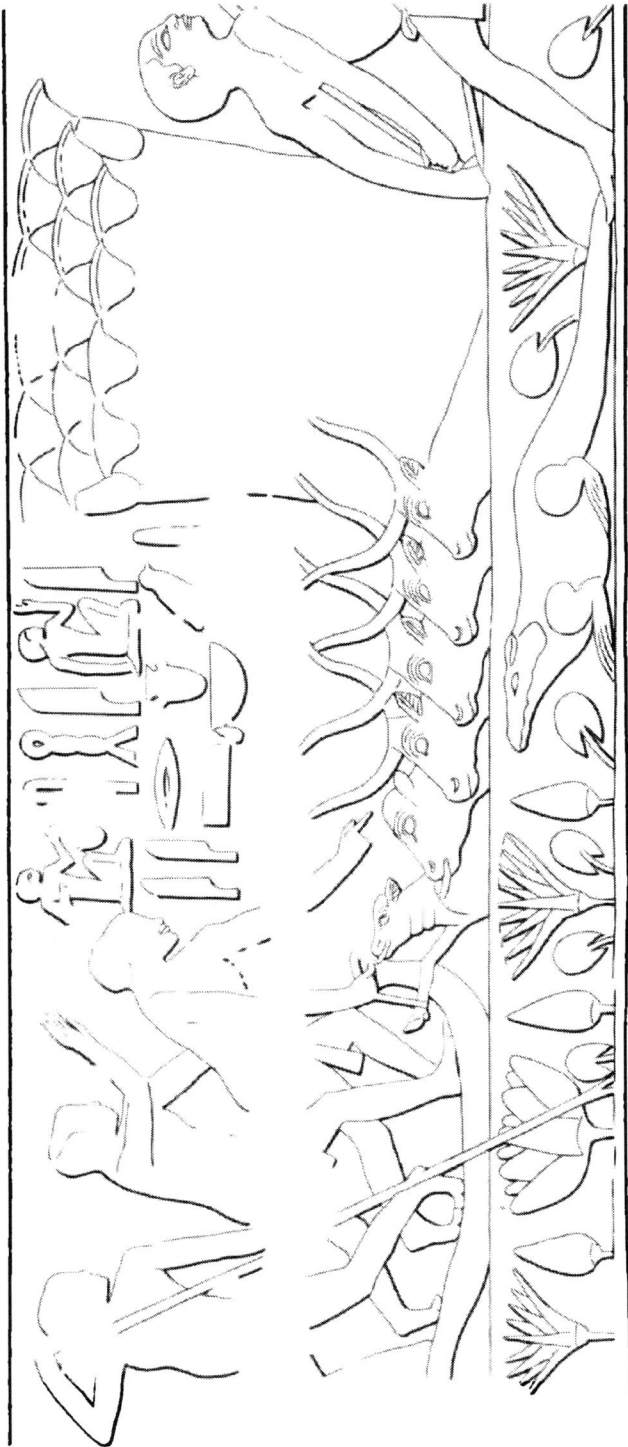

E. WALL (PL. XXXIII, E, R, A). *Scale ⅛.*

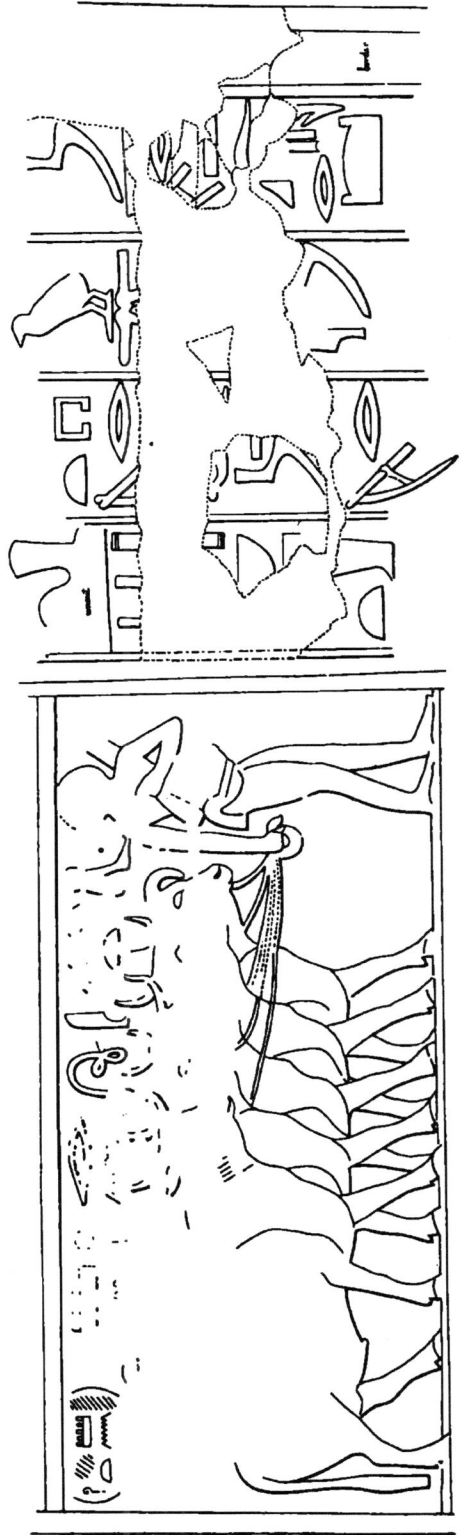

S. WALL (RESTORED). *Scale ⅛.*

E. SIDE OF DOORWAY. *Scale ⅛.*

1

2

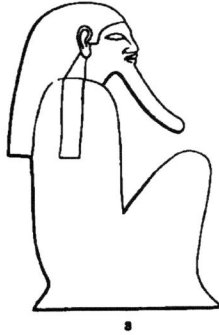

3

4

5

6

7

8

9

10

11

12

13

14

15

16

17

18

19

20

21

22

23

24

25

26

27

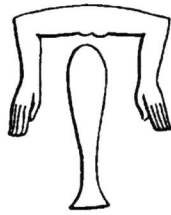
28

29

30

31

32

33

34

39

35

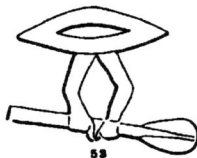
36

37

38

40

41

42

43

44

47

45

46

52

48

49

50

51

53

54

55

55

57

58

59

60

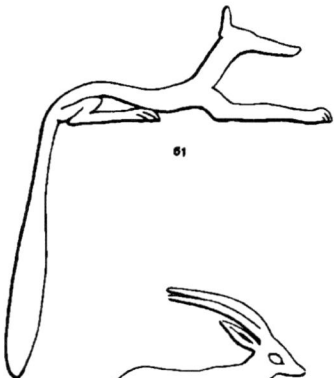

51

62

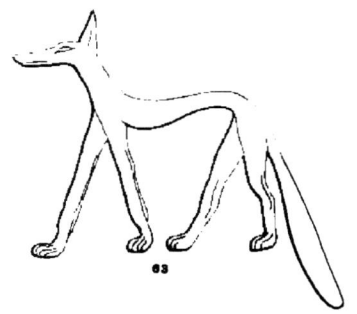

63

64

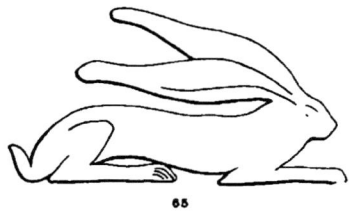

65

66

67

68

69

70

71

72

73

74

75

76

77

78

79

80

81

85

83

84

86

82

87

88   89

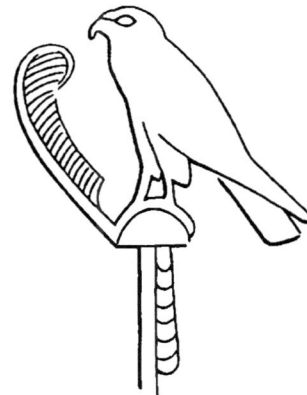

90

91

92

93

94

95

96

97

98

99

100

101

105

102

106

103

104

107

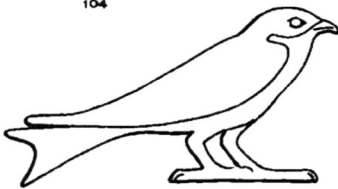

108

112

109

110

111

113

114

115

116

117

118

119

120

121

122

123

PLATE IX.

124

125

126

127

128

129

130

131

132

133

134

135

136

137

138

139

140

141

142

143

144

145

146

147

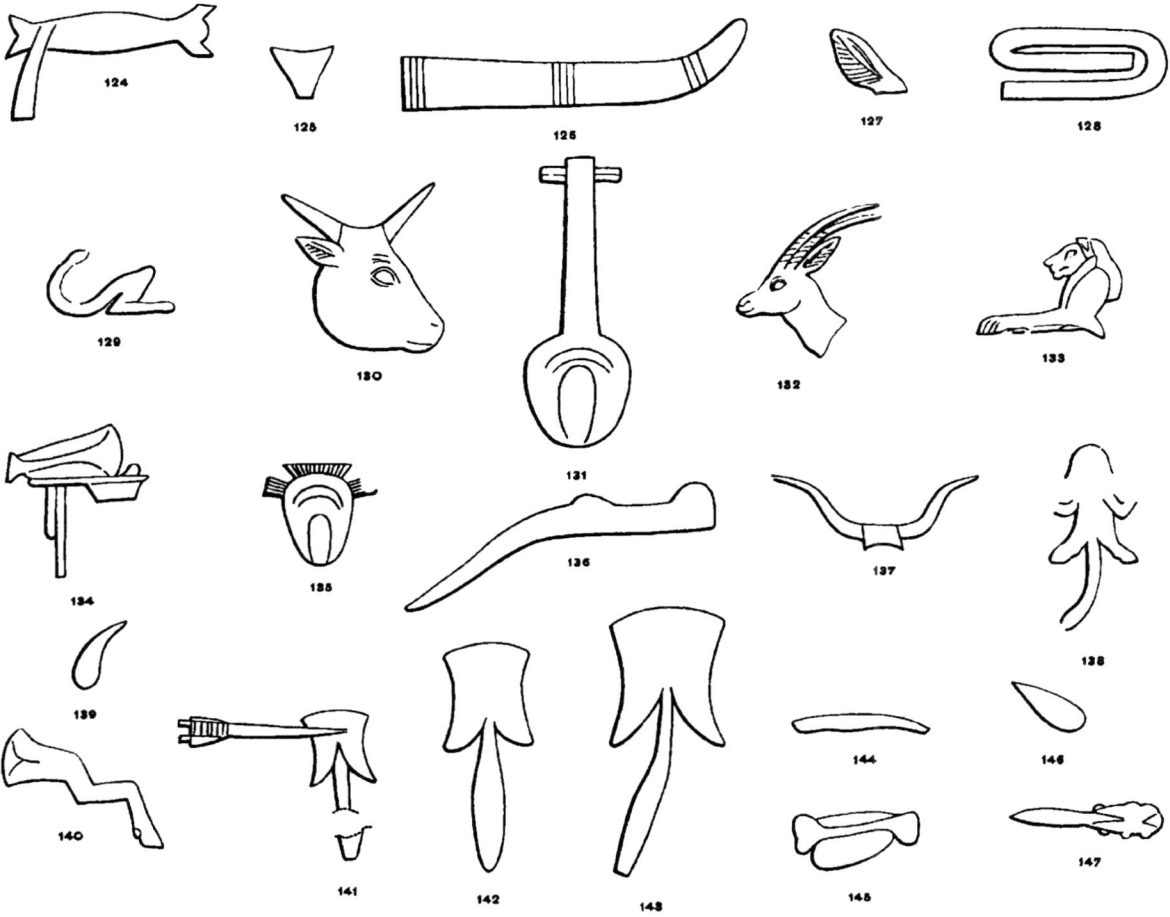

CLASS VI. LOWER ORDERS OF ANIMALS.

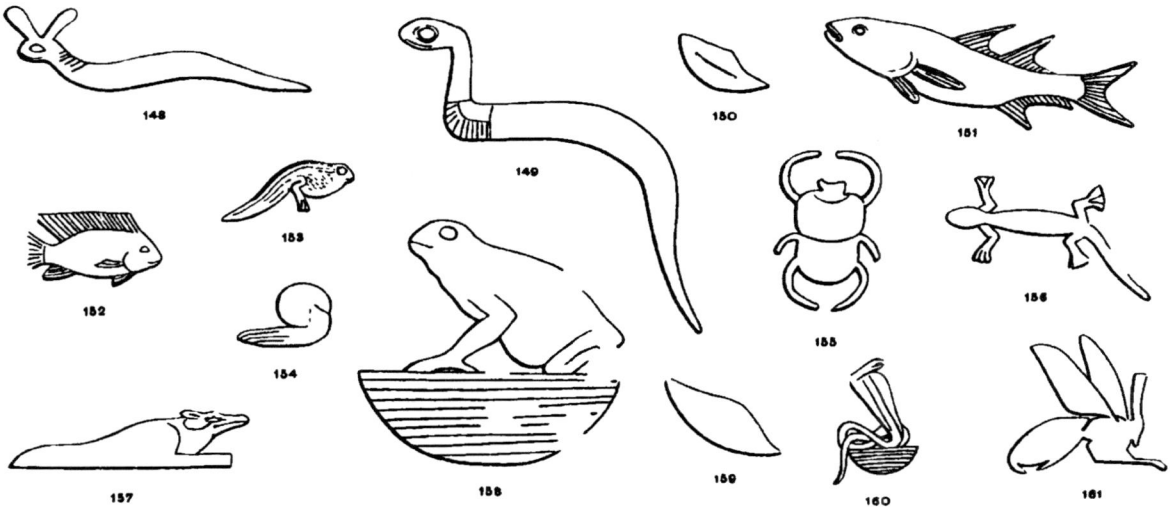

148

149

150

151

152

153

154

155

156

157

158

159

160

161

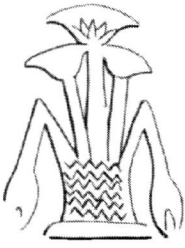

162

163

154

155

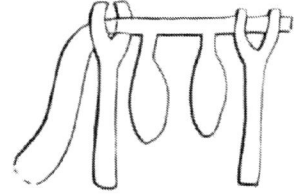

166

159

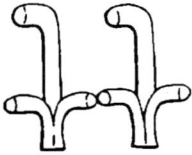

167

170

168

171

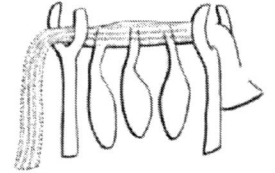

172

173

174

175

176

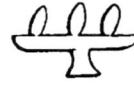

177

178

179

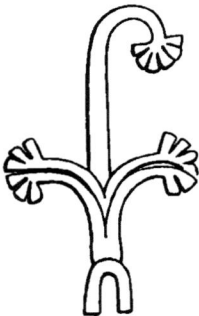

180

181

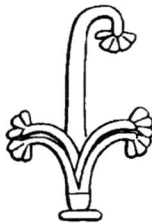

182

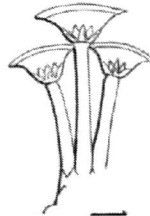

183

184

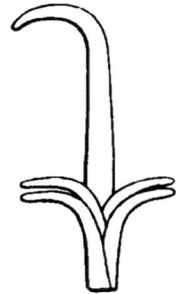

185

186

187

188

189

190

191

193

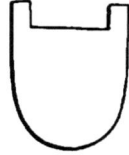

194

195

196

197

198

202

200

201

203

205

206

204

207

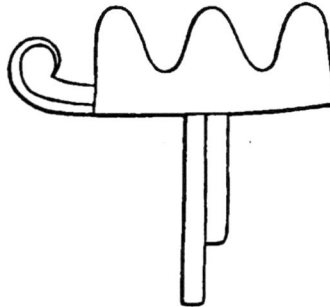

208

209

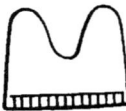

210

211

212

213

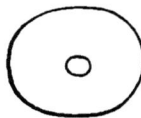

214

215

216

217

218

219

220

221

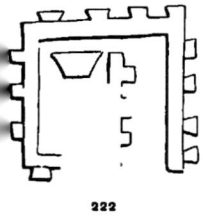

222

223

224

225

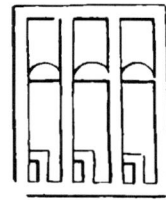

226

227

228

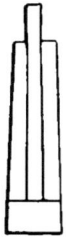

229

230

231

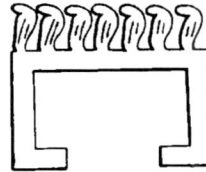

232

233

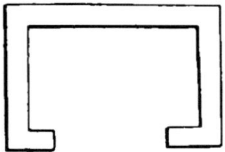

234

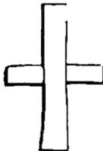

235

239b

236

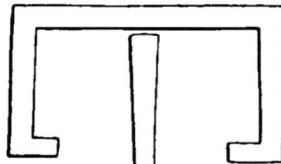

237

238

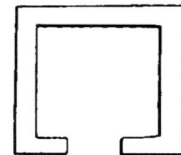

243

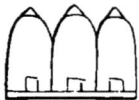

239

240

241

242

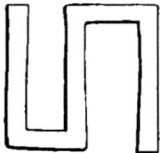

244

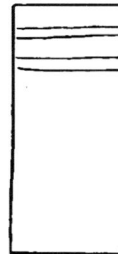

247

248

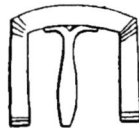

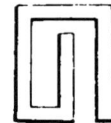

251

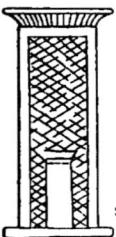

245

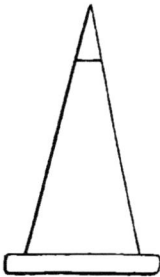

246

249

250

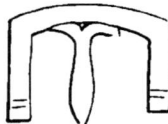

2

222

223

224

225

226

227

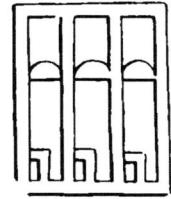

228

229

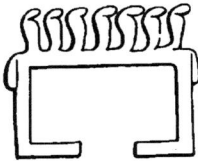

230

231

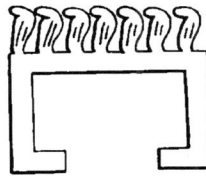

232

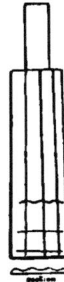

233

234

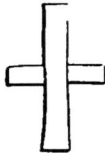

235

239b

240

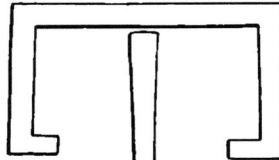

236

241

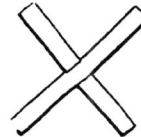

237

242

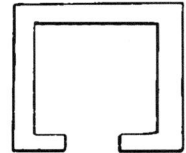

238

243

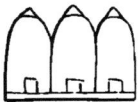

239

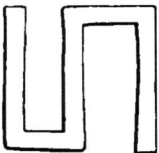

244

245

246

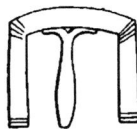

247

248

249

250

251

252

253

254

255

256

257

258

259

260

263

265

266

269

261

262

264

267

268

270

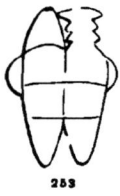

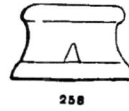

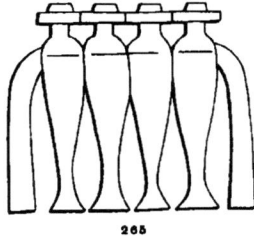

CLASS XI. IMPLEMENTS AND TOOLS.

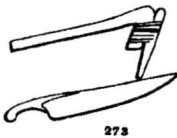

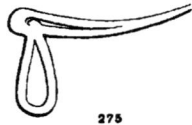

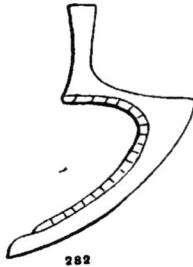

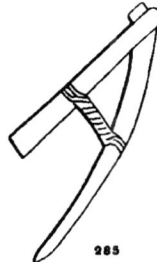

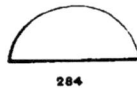

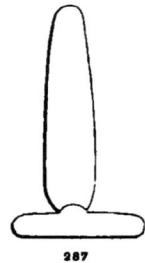

271   272   273

274

276

278

279

275

277

280

286

281

282

283

285

284

287

288

289

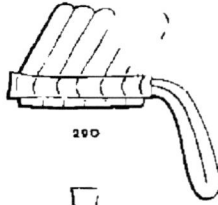

290

291

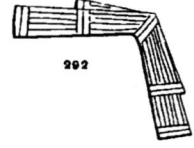

292

293

294

295

296

297

298

299

300

301

302

303

304

305

306

307

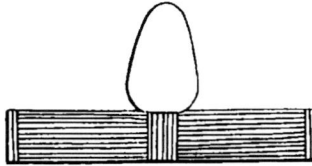

308

313

309

310

311

312

314

315

316

317

318

319

320

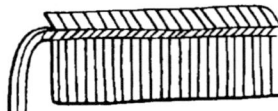

321

322

323

324

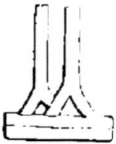

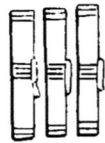
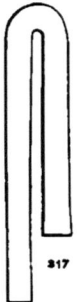

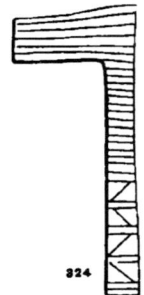

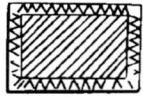

325

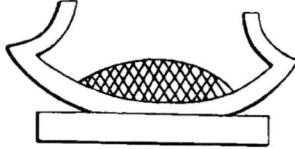

326

327

328

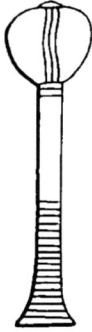

329

330

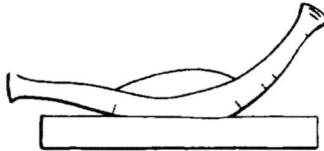

331

332

333

334

335

336

337

338

339

CLASS XIV. ARTICLES FOR PERSONAL USE, FURNITURE, FOOD, ETC.

340

341

343

342

345

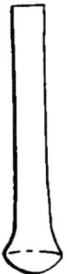

344

346

347

348

349

350

351

352

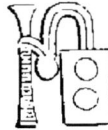

353

354

355

356

357

358

359

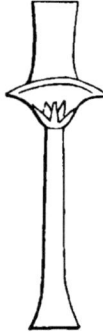

360

361

362

MISCELLANEOUS DETAILS.

Scale ½

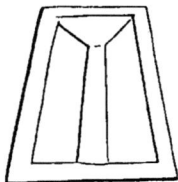

363

364

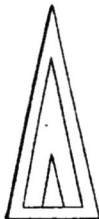

365

366

367

368

369

370

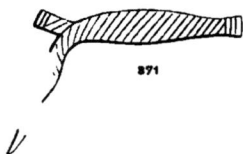

371

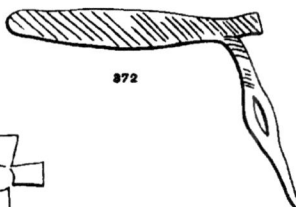

372

373

374

375

376

377

378

379

380

381

382

383

384

385

386

387

388

389

390

391

392

393

394

395

396

397

398

HUNTSMAN. PTAHHETEP, EAST WALL.   *Scale 1 : 2.*

399

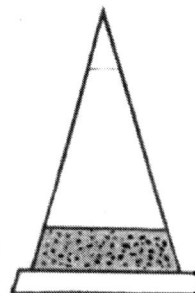

400

401

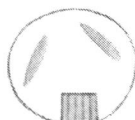

402

406

403

404

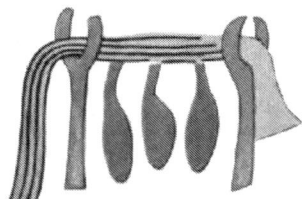

405

408

409

410

407

411

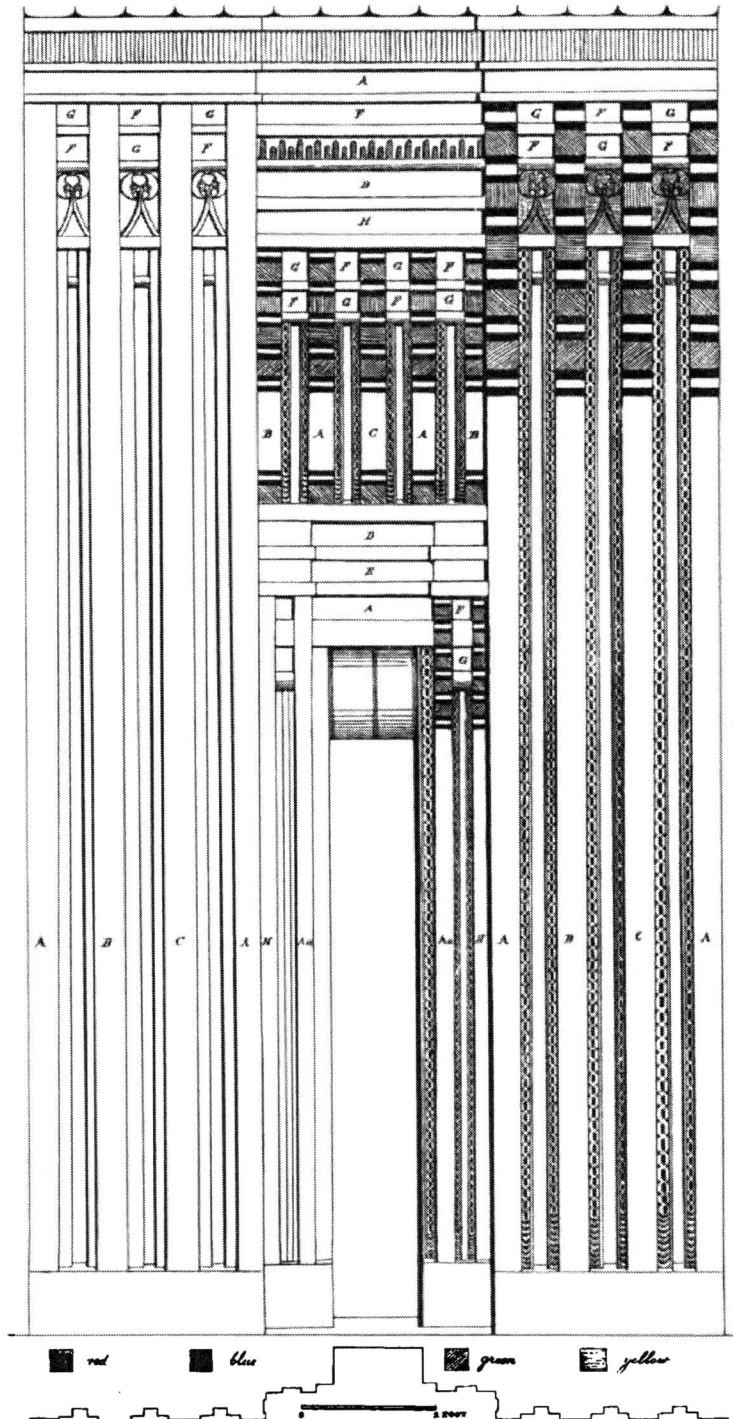

red   blue   green   yellow

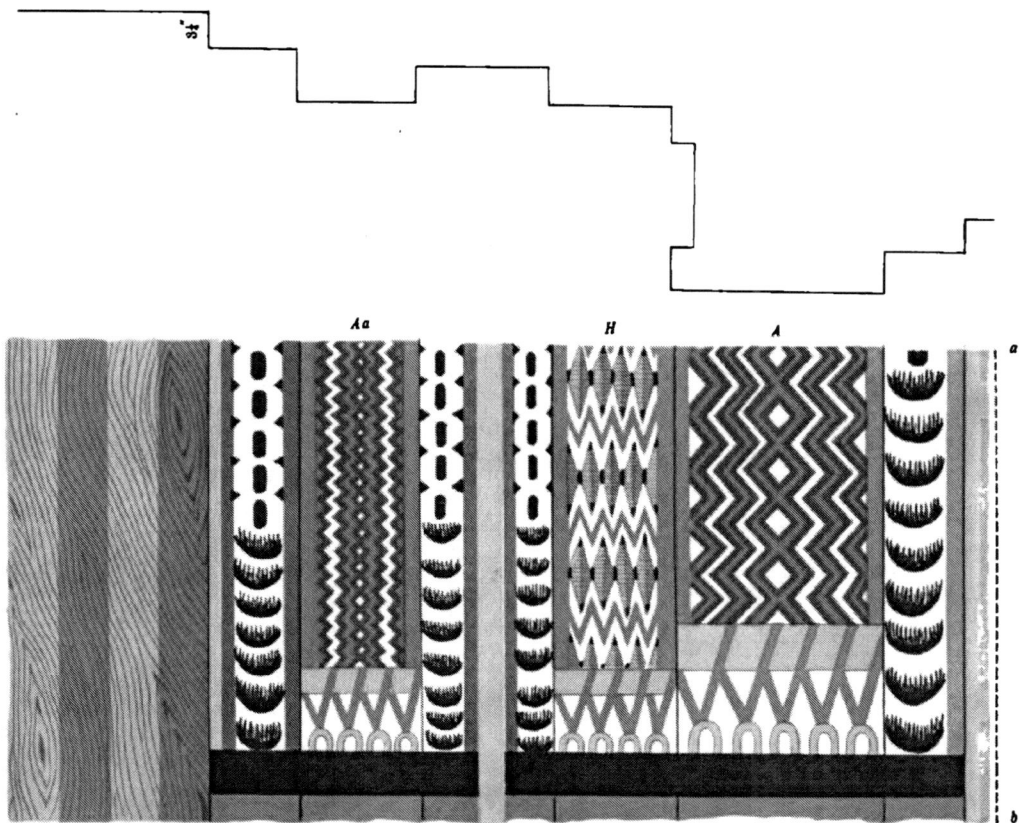

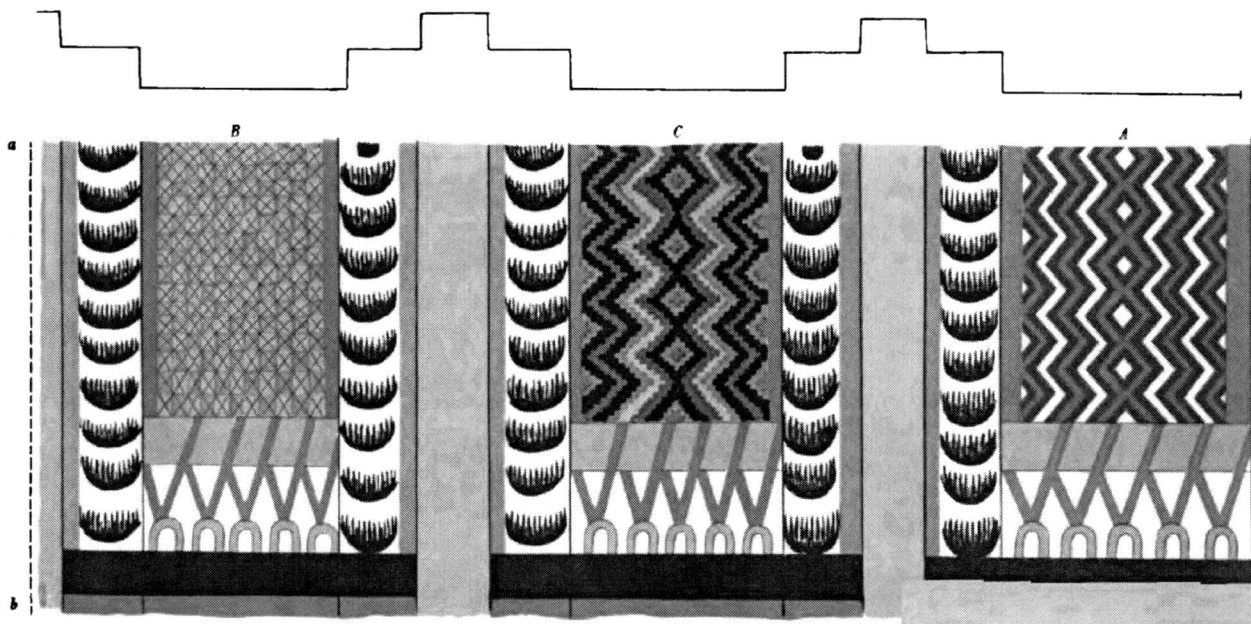

LOWER PORTION—RIGHT SIDE (*divided at a...b*).

Sca

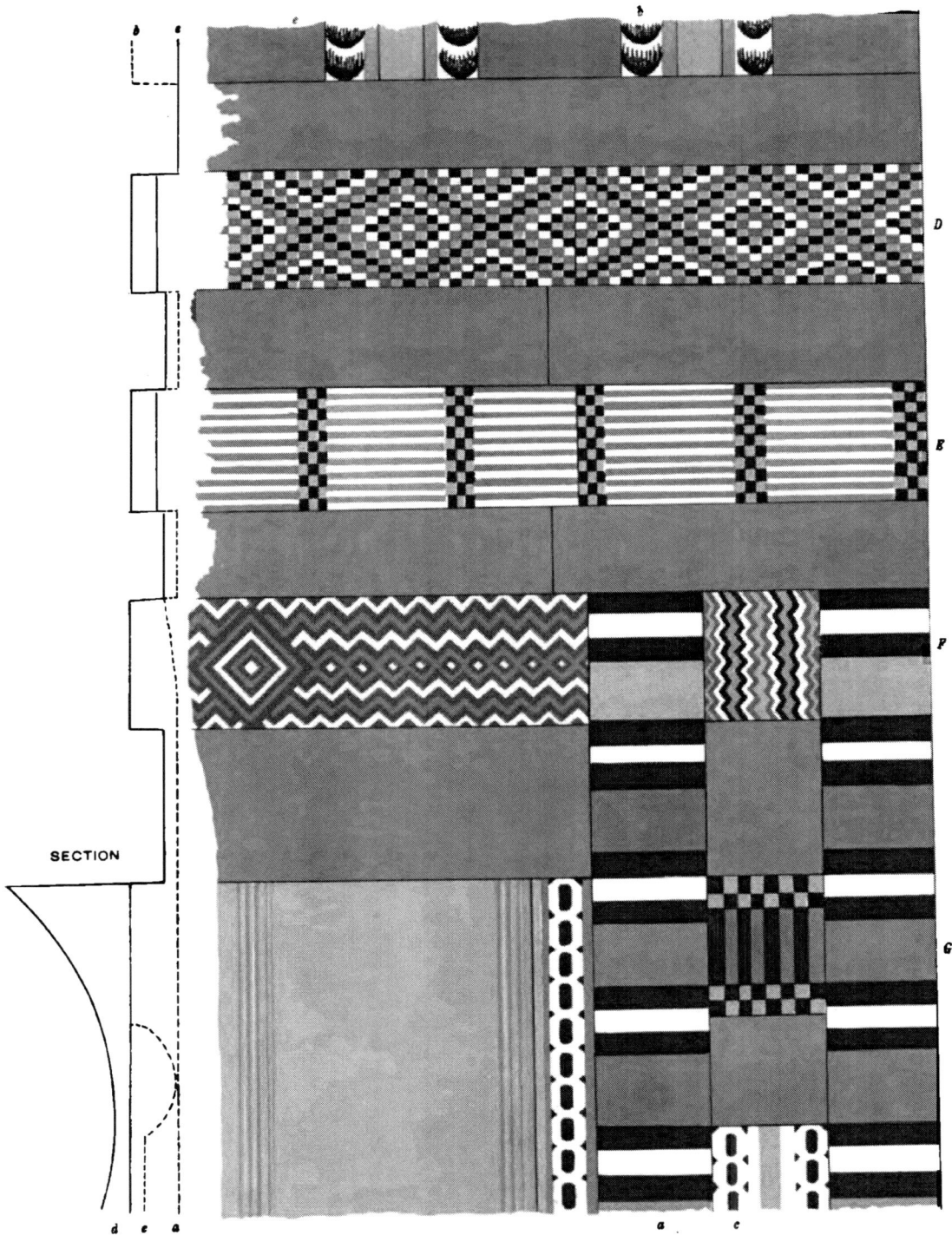

SECTION

D

E

F

G

CENTRE PORTION—RIGHT SIDE.

Scale ⅟

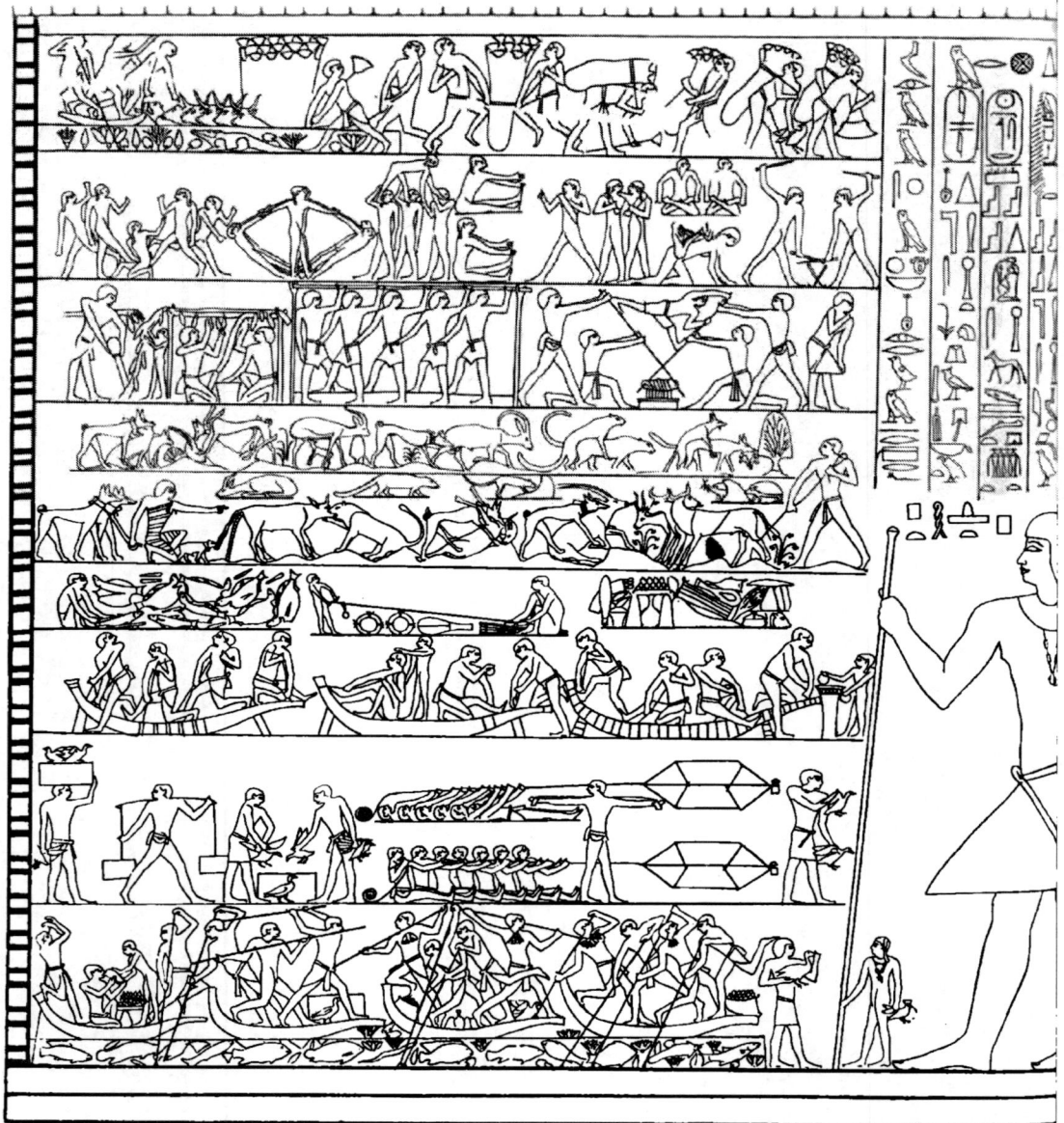

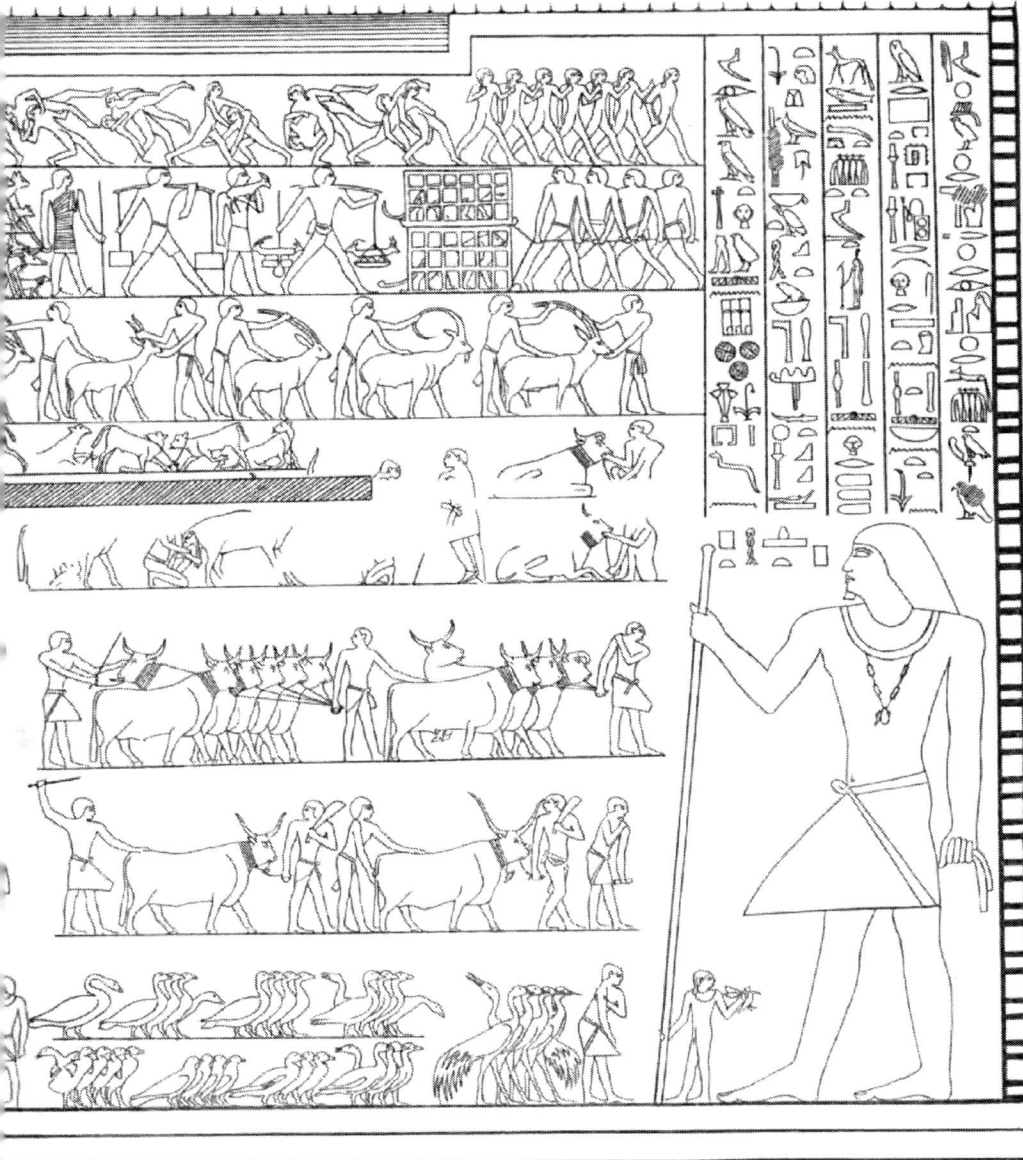

PLATE XXI.

Scale ½

WALL.

THE DEER—E

HUNTING IN THE D

PLATE XXII.

T WALL.

Scale ⅛

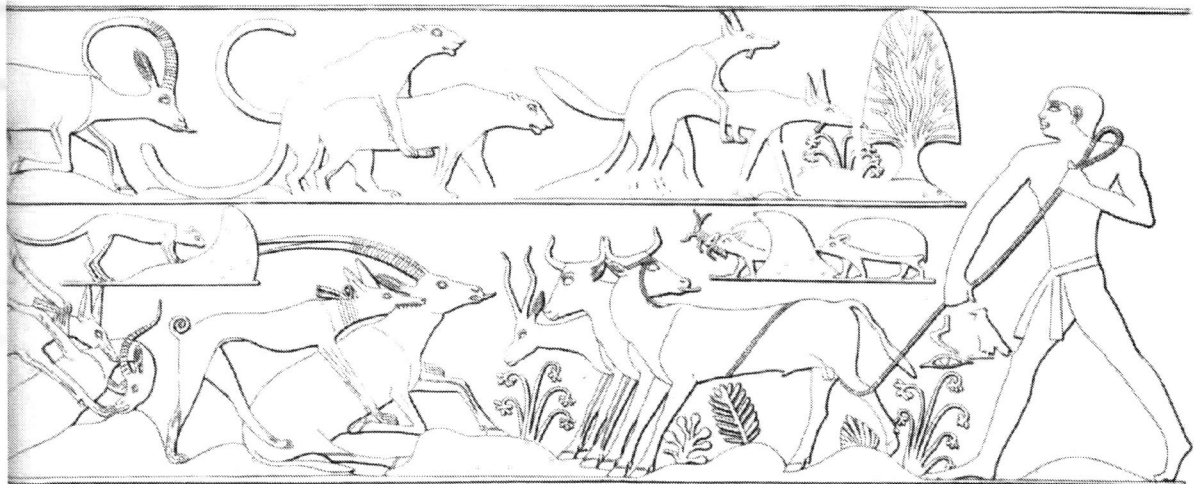

RT—EAST WALL.

Scale ⅛

PLATE XXIII

EAST WALL

UPPER REGISTERS — N. HALF

PLATE XXIV

EAST WALL

PHOTOTYP'E S.A.D.A.G. — GENÈVE

UPPER REGISTERS — S. HALF

PLATE XXV

EAST WALL

LOWER REGISTERS — N. HALF

PLATE XXVI

EAST WALL

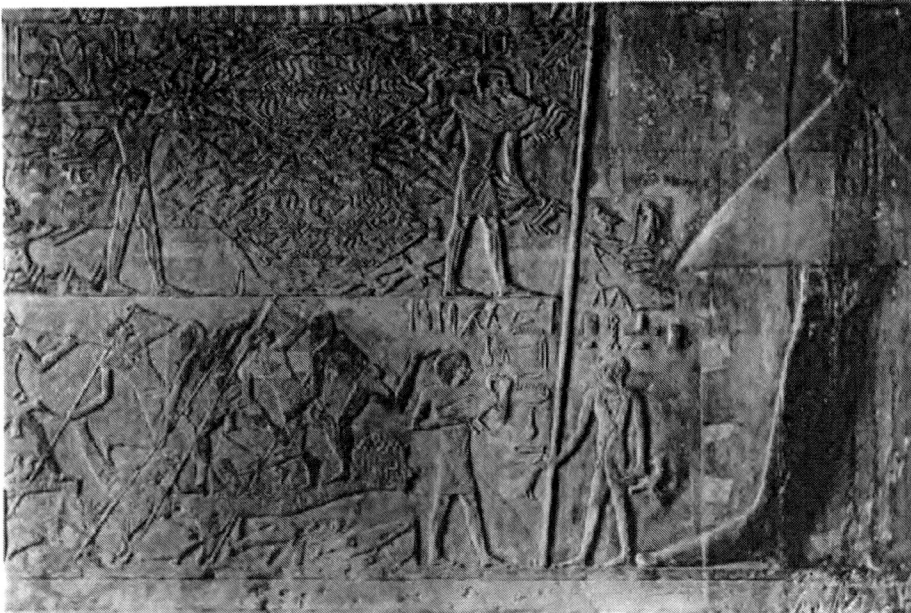

LOWER REGISTERS — N. HALF, continued.

PLATE XXVII

EAST WALL

PHOTOTYPIE S.A.D.A.G. — GENÈVE

LOWER REGISTERS — S. HALF

PLATE XXVIII

EAST WALL

PHOTOTYPIE S.A.D.A.G. — GENÈVE

LOWER REGISTERS — S. HALF, continued.

PLATE XXIX

WEST WALL

N. HALF

PHOTOTYPIE S.A.D.A.G. — GENÈVE

S. HALF

PLATE XXX

PHOTOTYPIE S.A.D.A.G. — GENÉVE

NORTH WALL